500 COLOR IDEAS FOR SMALL SPACES

500 IDÉES DE COULEURS POUR PETITS ESPACES

500 FARBIDEEN FÜR KLEINE RÄUME

EVERGREEN is an imprint of

Taschen GmbH

© 2007 TASCHEN GmbH

Hohenzollernring 53, D-50672 Köln

www.taschen.com

Editorial coordination:
Simone Schleifer

Editor:
Simone Schleifer, Daniela Santos Quartino

Editorial assistant:
Macarena San Martín, Esther Moreno

Text:
Daniela Santos Quartino

English translation:
Gene Ferber

French translation:
Marion Westerhoff

German translation:
Susanne Engler

Proofreading:
Ian Ayers, Cecile Cano, Martin Rolshoven

Art director:
Mireia Casanovas Soley

Graphic design and layout:
Oriol Serra Juncosa, Laura Millán

Printed in Spain

ISBN 978-3-8365-0096-8

500 COLOR IDEAS FOR SMALL SPACES
500 IDÉES DE COULEURS POUR PETITS ESPACES
500 FARBIDEEN FÜR KLEINE RÄUME

WITHDRAWN

evergreen

Contents Sommaire Inhalt

Color is one of the most effective tools in architecture and interior design. Thanks to its ability to transform, it can enlarge spaces, alter shapes, set off volumes, and divide or draw rooms together. It can also transmit light and warmth to the darkest corners, highlight or conceal structural building elements and emphasize the shapes of furnishings.

The great advantage of color is that dramatic changes need not involve major works nor cost a lot of money. Choosing the right color is all that is required in order to achieve the desired effect and instantly modify the character of the various living spaces and the ways of using them.

One of its most important aspects is the effect it has on a person's mood. Color has the power to contribute to the mental well-being of the occupants of a house. Harmonious and welcoming surroundings can be obtained with the application of one or two colors, or combinations of the two. This may be a matter of personal taste. However color, and how it is applied, cannot be left to chance. It is important to understand the language of color in order to be able to create one's own environment.

Conceived with small spaces in mind, this book focuses on color and how to make the most of it in reduced spaces. Readers will no doubt find the ideas and the hundreds of illustrations contained in this work a great source of inspiration and aid when having to make decisions about decoration.

From how to paint walls, ceilings and floors, to how to choose items of furniture and decorative accessories, the ideas presented here offer practical solutions for enlarging space and demonstrate that having a contemporary, stylish house is not a question of size.

La couleur est un des outils les plus efficaces de l'architecture et du design d'intérieur. Sa faculté de modification, lui permet d'agrandir l'espace, de moduler les formes et mettre les volumes en évidence, de séparer les pièces ou en unir d'autres. La couleur permet également de diffuser lumière et chaleur dans les chambres les plus sombres, d'exalter ou de dissimuler des éléments structuraux de construction et de valoriser les formes de l'équipement de la maison.

L'immense avantage de la couleur, c'est de susciter de grands changements sans aucun travaux ni frais majeurs. Il suffit de choisir le ton approprié pour réussir l'effet voulu et changer immédiatement le caractère et l'usage des espaces.

Un de ses effets majeurs est celui qui s'effectue sur l'état d'âme des personnes. La couleur a le pouvoir d'intervenir directement sur la qualité de vie des occupants d'un espace de vie. Les ambiances harmonieuses et accueillantes sont le fruit de l'application de l'une ou l'autre couleur et de ses associations. Le choix des couleurs, bien que déterminé par le goût personnel, ne peut cependant pas être laissé au hasard. Pour cela, la connaissance du langage des couleurs est un passage obligatoire pour tous ceux qui désirent créer leur environnement personnel.

Cet ouvrage est conçu pour tirer le meilleur parti de la couleur en se concentrant sur les habitations comptant peu de mètres carrés. Grâce à toutes ces idées et aux centaines d'illustrations qui les accompagnent, le lecteur trouvera dans ce volume une source d'inspiration d'une importance clé au moment de prendre les petites et grandes décisions en matière de décoration.

Dans l'art et la manière de peindre murs, plafonds et sols, jusqu'au type de meubles et accessoires décoratifs, les idées présentées ici offrent des solutions pratiques pour agrandir visuellement l'espace et démontrent qu'une maison moderne et pleine de style n'a pas forcément besoin de beaucoup de surface.

Die Farbe ist eines der effektivsten Gestaltungsmittel in der Architektur und Innenarchitektur. Farben haben die Fähigkeit zu verändern. Deshalb kann man durch ihre geschickte Verwendung Räume größer wirken lassen, Formen verändern oder betonen, Räume trennen oder vereinen. Ebenso lassen Farben dunkle Räume heller und wärmer wirken. Sie verbergen oder heben strukturelle Elemente des Gebäudes hervor und betonen die Formen der Wohnungseinrichtung.

Der große Vorteil von Farben ist, dass man ohne umfassende und teure Baumaßnahmen große Veränderungen erreicht. Es genügt, den geeigneten Farbton zu wählen, um die beabsichtigte Wirkung zu erzielen. So kann man das Aussehen und die Art der Raumnutzung schnell und einfach verändern.

Eine der wichtigsten Wirkungen der Farben ist der Einfluss, den sie auf den Gemütszustand des Menschen haben. Die Farben besitzen die Macht, direkt die Lebensqualität der Bewohner einer Wohnung oder eines Hauses zu beeinflussen. Man kann durch die Verwendung verschiedener Farben und Farbkombinationen harmonische und einladende Wohnumgebungen schaffen. Aber man sollte die Farbauswahl nicht einfach dem Zufall überlassen, auch wenn sie natürlich Geschmackssache ist und somit eine sehr persönliche Entscheidung. Es ist wichtig, die Sprache der Farben zu kennen, vor allem wenn man seine eigene Wohnung gestalten möchte. Dieses Buch wurde mit dem Ziel verfasst, die optimalen Farben für kleinere Wohnungen und Häuser zu zeigen. Dieser Band stellt mit seinen vielen Ideen und Fotos eine umfassende Informationsquelle dar und hilft dem Leser dabei, kleinere und größere Entscheidungen bezüglich der Einrichtung und Dekoration zu treffen.

Es wird gezeigt, wie man Wände, Decken und Böden farblich gestalten kann, und welche Art von Möbeln oder Dekorationselementen gut dazu passen. Die Ideen, die in diesem Band zusammengestellt wurden, bieten praktische Lösungen, um Räume optisch zu vergrößern, und sie beweisen, dass auch kleine Wohnungen oder Häuser sehr modern und stilvoll gestaltet werden können.

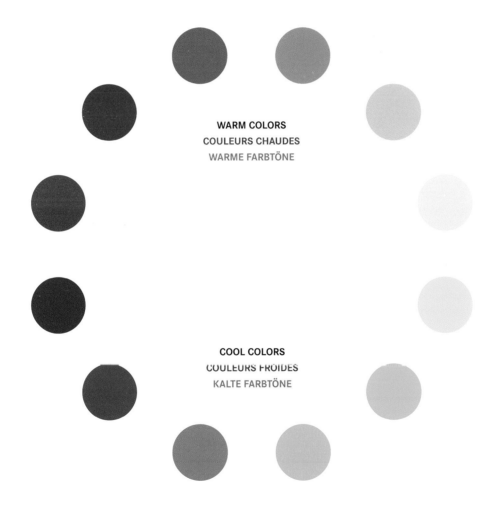

WARM COLORS
COULEURS CHAUDES
WARME FARBTÖNE

COOL COLORS
COULEURS FROIDES
KALTE FARBTÖNE

Yellow Jaune **Gelb** Ocher Ocres
Ockertöne Dark Green Vert foncé
Dunkelgrün Light Green Vert
clair **Hellgrün** Blue Bleu **Blau**
Turquoise Turquoise **Türkis** Violet
Violet **Violett** Magenta Magenta
Magenta Pink Rose **Rosa** Red
Rouge **Rot** Orange Orange **Orange**
Brown Marron **Braun** Black Noir
Schwarz White Blanc **Weiß** Gray
Gris **Grau** Gold Or **Gold** Silver
Argent **Silber** Multicolor Multicolore
Bunt Transparencies Transparences
Transparenz Yellow Jaune **Gelb**
Ocher Ocres **Ockertöne** Dark Green

Colors
Couleurs
Farben

Colors arouse feelings, produce sensations, affect moods, encourage certain activities and induce relaxation. Their presence defines the character of a living space, shapes its style and reveals the occupant's personality. There are no hard and fast rules for their application. But it is necessary to take into account certain guidelines deeply rooted in culture and in the psychology of sensory perception – our brain's responses to various light stimulants – in order to make the right decision when creating the type of environment we want for our own private universe.

Les couleurs éveillent des sensations, provoquent des états d'âmes, favorisent certaines activités ou facilitent le repos. Leur présence définit le caractère des espaces, en dessine le style et révèle la personnalité de ses occupants. Il est important de savoir qu'il n'y a pas de formules invariables pour l'appliquer. Mais il faut bien sûr tenir compte de quelques règles enracinées dans la culture et dans la psychologie de la perception sensorielle – notre cerveau réagit devant les différentes stimulations lumineuses –, pour prendre la bonne décision à l'heure de décider l'environnement que nous voulons créer dans notre univers privé.

Farben erwecken Gefühle, beeinflussen die Stimmung, regen zu bestimmten Aktivitäten an und entspannen. Farben definieren den Charakter und Stil der Räume und sie verraten viel über die Persönlichkeit ihrer Bewohner. Für die Anwendung der Farben existieren zahllose Möglichkeiten – und nicht nur einige unveränderliche Regeln. Jedoch sollte man gewisse Richtlinien berücksichtigen, die kulturell bedingt sind oder auf die Psychologie der Sinneswahrnehmungen zurückgehen, denn unser Gehirn reagiert unterschiedlich auf gewisse Lichtreize. So kann man die richtige Entscheidung für die Wohnumgebungen treffen, die man in seinem privaten Universum schaffen möchte.

051

001

Yellow
Jaune
Gelb

007

001 Yellow is the warmest, most luminous and extroverted of colors. Its presence in the house denotes an atmosphere that is both youthful and vibrant.
Le jaune est la couleur la plus lumineuse, chaude et expansive. Sa présence dans la maison affiche des ambiances juvéniles et pleines de vie.
Gelb ist die leuchtendste, wärmste und expansivste Farbe. Die Farbe Gelb macht die Wohnumgebung jung und sehr lebendig.

002 This color evokes strength and willpower. Because of its strong stimulating effect it is best used in rooms that do not receive a lot of light.
Cette couleur évoque force et volonté. Stimulante, elle est davantage appropriée pour les chambres faiblement éclairées.
Diese Farbe lässt den Eindruck von Kraft und starkem Willen entstehen. Sie ist anregend und sollte vor allem in Zimmern verwendet werden, in denen es wenig Licht gibt.

003 Yellow was the symbol of the Emperor of China and, as such, a symbol of the Chinese monarchy. In the world of the theater, it is supposed to bring bad luck because Molière was wearing this colour when he died during the performance of his work *The Imaginary Invalid*.
La couleur jaune était le symbole de l'empereur de Chine et, par conséquent, de la monarchie chinoise. Par contre, au théâtre, elle porte malheur : en effet, Molière est mort vêtu de cette même couleur, alors qu'il jouait son oeuvre, *Le malade imaginaire*.
Die Farbe Gelb war das Symbol des Kaisers von China und deshalb auch der chinesischen Monarchie. In der Welt des Theaters existiert der Aberglaube, dass Gelb Unglück bringt, da Molière zum Zeitpunkt seines Todes in dieser Farbe gekleidet war, während er sein Werk „Der eingebildete Kranke" aufführte.

004 It is ideal for creating a feeling of space in small rooms, but only lighte tones should be used as a very bright yellow can become somewha overpowering.
Elle est idéale pour créer une sensation d'espace dans les petits vol mes, mais seulement si elle est appliquée dans sa gamme plus claire. L jaune criard peut devenir légèrement étouffant.
Ideal, um kleine Räume größer wirken zu lassen, allerdings sollte ma dazu zarte Gelbtöne verwenden. Ein zu grelles Gelb kann erdrücker wirken.

005 A warm, gentle yellow is easy to combine with other colors. It is suitab for those areas in the house meant for rest or entertainment, such a bedrooms or sitting rooms.
Dans une teinte plus chaude, le jaune est une couleur facile à combine Il est idéal pour les espaces de vie relaxants et accueillants, comm chambres à coucher et salons.
Die warmen Gelbtöne sind einfach zu kombinieren. Die Farbe eignet si ausgezeichnet für entspannte und gemütliche Umgebungen wie Schla und Wohnzimmer.

006 White door and window frames set against yellow walls are reminisce of Spanish colonial styles, of which Mexican haciendas are a particul example, complemented by natural-wood furniture.
Les cadres blancs des portes et des fenêtres sur des murs jaunes re voient aux styles coloniaux qui, à l'instar des grandes propriétés mex caines, s'agrémentent de mobilier de bois de couleur naturelle.

008

010

Weiße Tür- und Fensterrahmen in gelben Wänden sind typisch für den Kolonialstil, der, wie in den mexikanischen Häusern, mit naturfarbenen Holzmöbeln kombiniert wird.

007 Yellow is also considered one of the primary colors typical of Mediterranean regions, such as Provence. It is often used to give warmth to rather cool surroundings.

Le jaune est également considéré comme une couleur provençale, c'est à dire, primaire et typiquement méditerranéenne. Elle s'emploie fréquemment pour rendre les pièces froides chaleureuses.

Gelb wird auch als die Farbe der Provence betrachtet, also eine typische und häufige Farbe im Mittelmeerraum. Die Farbe wird häufig in kalten Räumen verwendet, um diese wärmer wirken zu lassen.

008 It is a perfect element a house in which white is the dominant color. Painting the wall that faces the main source of natural light yellow creates a soft atmosphere without altering the character of the house.

C'est un élément idéal dans les habitations où le blanc prédomine. En peignant de jaune le mur opposé à l'entrée principale de lumière naturelle, on obtient une ambiance douce qui n'altère en rien le caractère de la maison.

Eine ideale Farbe für Wohnungen, in denen Weiß dominiert. Wenn man die Wand, die dem Fenster gegenüber liegt und durch die das meiste Licht fällt, gelb streicht, entsteht eine sanfte Atmosphäre, die den Charakter des Hauses nicht verändert.

009 Painting high ceilings in a pale yellow color, in contrast with the white of the walls, will visually reduce their height.

Dans les maisons à très hauts plafonds, les peindre en jaune clair et les murs en blanc, permet de les diminuer visuellement.

In sehr hohen Räumen kann man die Decke optisch niedriger machen, indem man sie hellgelb und die Wände weiß streicht.

010 Metallic yellow is a favourite color for recreating 'vintage' environments.

Dans sa version métallisée, c'est une des couleurs privilégiées pour recréer des ambiances *vintage*.

Metallisches Gelb wird gerne benutzt, um die Umgebung heiter wirken zu lassen.

011 Yellow is one of the very few colors that, together with white, can be used throughout the house. The trick is to combine different kinds of yellows in each area.

C'est une des rares couleurs qui, comme le blanc, peut s'utiliser dans toute la maison. Le secret est d'associer différents tons de jaune dans chacun des espaces de celle-ci.

Es handelt sich um eine der wenigen Farben, die neben Weiß im ganzen Haus benutzt werden kann. Dabei ist es entscheidend, dass verschiedene Gelbtöne in jedem der Räume miteinander kombiniert werden.

012 Yellow carpets are perfect for counteracting the overwhelming presence of white in minimalist surroundings.

Les moquettes de cette couleur sont idéales pour contrecarrer l'hégémonie du blanc dans les univers minimalistes.

Teppichböden in Gelb eignen sich hervorragend, um die Vorherrschaft der Farbe Weiß in minimalistisch gestalteten Räumen zu brechen.

012

002

Ocher
Ocres
Ockertöne

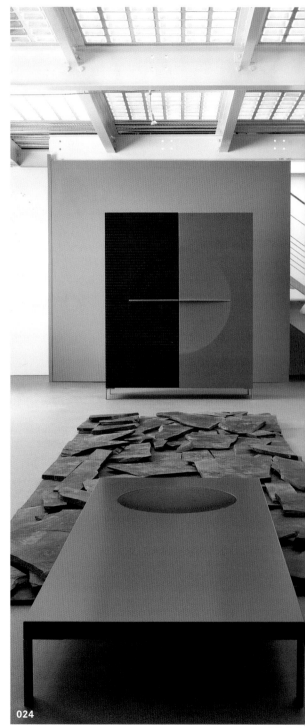

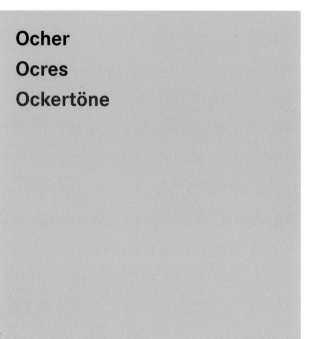

015

024

021

013 Ochers are among the oldest pigments in existence. They were already used for murals and constructions in prehistoric times. Jean-Etienne Astier made the color ocher popular when he started producing it on a large scale in the French city of Roussillon in 1785.
Les ocres appartiennent aux pigments les plus anciens. On les utilisait déjà à la préhistoire pour les fresques et les constructions. Cette couleur obtient un regain de popularité lorsqu'en 1785, Jean-Etienne Astier commence à les produire à grande échelle, dans la ville de Roussillon, en France.
Ockertöne werden mit den ältesten bekannten Pigmenten hergestellt. Bereits in der Vorgeschichte wurden sie für Wandmalereien und Bauten benutzt. Diese Farbe gewann an Beliebtheit, als Jean-Étienne Astier im Jahr 1785 in der französischen Stadt Roussillon damit begann, sie in großen Mengen herzustellen.

014 Due to its composition, ocher is associated with reds, yellows and browns, belonging therefore to the category of warm colors.
Selon leur composition, ils existent dans les tons rouge, jaune ou marron, se situant ainsi dans la gamme des couleurs chaudes.
Je nach der Zusammensetzung kann man die Farbe Ocker in rötlicher, gelblicher oder bräunlicher Version finden, so dass sie zu den so genannten warmen Farben gehört.

015 Thanks to their great light reflecting properties ochers are ideal for creating a feeling of space in naturally dark surroundings.
De par leur grande capacité de réflexion de la lumière, les ocres sont idéales pour amplifier les pièces naturellement sombres.

Da Ocker das Licht sehr gut reflektiert, eignet es sich ideal, um dunkle Räume größer wirken zu lassen.

016 These shades go very well with the browns and blacks of the kind of furniture usually found in any room.
Ces couleurs se conjuguent à merveille aux marron et noir des meubles typiques que l'on trouve habituellement dans les pièces.
Ockertöne passen ausgezeichnet zu den typischen Braun- und Schwarztönen der Möbel, die man in verschiedenen Räumen findet.

017 They are strongly recommended for bedrooms, as they create a warm, comfortable and relaxing atmosphere.
Il est particulièrement recommandé de l'employer dans les chambres, où il permet de créer une ambiance confortable et relaxante.
Die Farbe Ocker ist auch für Schlafzimmer gut geeignet, da sie eine einladende und entspannte Atmosphäre schafft.

018 Ochers are suitable for indigenous-style houses decorated with African art pieces.
Les ocres sont parfaites pour les maisons de style ethnique, décorées d'objets d'origine africaine.
Ockertöne passen auch ausgezeichnet zu Häusern, die im ethnischen Stil mit afrikanischen Elementen dekoriert sind.

019 Ocher-colored bamboo screens and sliding doors make this tint a favorite of Zen-inspired interiors.
Appliqué sur des paravents et portes coulissantes en bambou, c'est une des couleurs les plus utilisées dans les intérieurs d'inspiration zen.

017

014

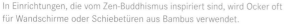

In Einrichtungen, die vom Zen-Buddhismus inspiriert sind, wird Ocker oft für Wandschirme oder Schiebetüren aus Bambus verwendet.

020 Natural fiber carpets and rugs in which ocher is the predominant tone are a practical option, giving a contemporary touch to dining rooms and lounges.

Les moquettes et tapis de fibre naturelle, où cette couleur prédomine, se révèlent être une option pratique qui confère un air contemporain aux salles à manger et salons.

Teppichböden oder Teppiche aus Naturfasern, bei denen die Farbe Ocker vorherrscht, sind eine praktische Lösung, die Speise- und Wohnzimmer zeitgemäß wirken lässt.

021 Ocher is often the natural color of both tiled and wooden floors, the former imparting a Mediterranean touch, and the latter a northern European style.

L'ocre est la couleur naturelle des sols de terre cuite ou de bois. Selon les cas, elle apporte un air méditerranéen ou un style nordique.

Ocker ist die natürliche Farbe von Terrakotta- oder Holzböden. Ockerfarbene Terrakottaböden wirken mediterran, Holzböden in der gleichen Farbe nordisch.

022 Strong colors such as brown or burgundy can be used for the walls in reduced spaces if ocher rugs or curtains are included in the decoration.

Il n'est pas nécessaire de renoncer aux couleurs intenses comme le marron ou le bordeaux sur les murs des petits espaces, si les tapis et rideaux sont de couleur ocre.

Man kann in kleinen Räumen durchaus Farben wie Braun oder Bordeaux für die Wände verwenden, wenn man diese mit ockerfarbenen Teppichen oder Gardinen kombiniert.

023 Ocher upholstered furniture offers a classic, enduring look that blends well with any kind of surrounding, regardless of the current fashion.

Les meubles tapissés de cette couleur ont un air classique qui les fait perdurer au-delà des modes, car ils sont faciles à combiner avec n'importe quel type d'ambiance.

Möbel, die in dieser Farbe bezogen sind, wirken klassisch und zeitlos. Sie lassen sich einfach mit jeder Art von Einrichtung kombinieren.

024 Combined with gray, ocher makes for one of the most elegant compositions. It is perfect with leather or chromed metal furniture.

Son association avec le gris, engendre une composition des plus élégantes : elle est parfaite pour les espaces de vie décorés de meubles conjuguant cuir et métal.

Ocker in Kombination mit Grau wirkt sehr elegant und eignet sich ausgezeichnet für Räume mit Leder- und Metallmöbeln.

Dark Green
Vert foncé
Dunkelgrün

036

025

025 Together with blue, green is one of the prominent colors of our plane The fact that it is immediately associated with nature makes it a tru agreeable tint for the decoration of the house.

Le vert est, avec le bleu, une des couleurs prédominantes de notre pl nète. L'association immédiate de cette couleur avec la nature procu une sensation de bien-être dans la maison.

Dunkelgrün und Blau sind die Farben, die auf unserem Planeten vc herrschen. Die unmittelbare Assoziation dieser Farbe mit der Nat führt dazu, dass man sie innerhalb eines Hauses als sehr angeneh empfindet.

026 A lead-and-oil-based paint used in the Victorian era made dark green t typical color of that time. Dark green has become synonymous wi sober and strongly masculine surroundings, especially in combinatio with dark wood furniture.

C'est la couleur typique de l'époque victorienne : une peinture réalisée base de plomb et d'huile qui s'utilisait alors. Ce vert anglais s'assoc avec les ambiances sobres et très masculines équipées de meubles bois sombre.

Dunkelgrün ist die typische Farbe des viktorianischen Zeitalters, was a die Bleifarbe mit Öl zurückzuführen ist, die man in dieser Epoche ve wendete. Deshalb verbindet man das Englischgrün auch mit schlicht und sehr männlichen Umgebungen, die mit dunklen Holzmöbeln dek riert sind.

027 The neobaroque trend has made this color fashionable again. Its use small spaces is quite acceptable and it goes particularly well with pi or white walls and accessories.

026

La tendance néo-baroque a remis cette couleur au goût du jour : elle peut s'employer sans crainte dans les petits espaces en alternance avec des murs ou accessoires roses ou blancs.

Der Trend zum Neobarock hat diese Farbe wieder aufgewertet. Man kann sie auch in kleinen Räumen verwenden, wenn man sie mit Wänden oder Dekorationselementen in den Farben Rosa oder Weiß abwechselt.

28 Conjuring up the image of a well-tended lawn, a dark-green carpet will make a house with large bay windows refreshingly cool.

Une moquette de cette couleur pour le sol d'une pièce vitrée, génère une sensation de fraîcheur grâce à l'association immédiate avec le gazon.

Ein dunkelgrüner Toppichboden in einem verglasten Raum wirkt sehr frisch, da diese Kombination an einen Rasen erinnert.

9 Choosing intense green for upholstery or deep-pile rugs can also induce a pleasurable feeling of being surrounded by lush countryside.

Les moquettes vertes ou les tapis à longs poils, dans un ton de vert intense, donnent également le sentiment d'être en pleine campagne.

Ebenso erweckt die Kombination von grünen Bezügen mit langhaarigen Teppichen in intensiven Farben das Gefühl, sich mitten in der Natur zu befinden.

0 Dark green is a good option for accessories. An attractive crystal vase in this shade, for example, will give an elegant touch to any surrounding.

Le vert foncé est une bonne solution pour les accessoires. Par exemple, un vase en verre de cette teinte, bien mis en évidence, imprègne toutes les atmosphères d'une touche d'élégance.

Dunkelgrün ist eine Farbe, die sich ausgezeichnet für Dekorationselemente eignet. So lässt zum Beispiel ein schöner Kristallkrug in dieser Farbe jede Umgebung elegant wirken.

031 This color helps reduce volumes and, applied with a silky finish, diminishes the size of furniture in small rooms.

Cette couleur, appliquée avec une patine, contribuera à réduire les volumes, et permet ainsi de masquer la taille des meubles dans les petites pièces.

Diese Farbe trägt dazu bei, die Formen kleiner wirken zu lassen. Wenn man sie als Patina aufträgt, wirken die Möbel in kleinen Räumen ebenfalls kleiner.

032 In a small house a bottle-green glass partition will help separate the dining-room area from the lounge, while still allowing the light to filter through.

Pour diviser le salon de la salle à manger d'une petite pièce, il est judicieux d'installer un mur en verre couleur vert bouteille : en effet, tout en séparant les zones de vie, il laisse passer la lumière.

Um das Wohnzimmer in einer kleinen Wohnung vom Speisezimmer abzutrennen, stellt eine flaschengrüne Trennwand aus Glas eine gute Lösung dar. So schafft man zwei unabhängige Räume; gleichzeitig fällt jedoch das Licht ein.

033 A green-paper band outlined with gold on an off-white wall will help create a small baroque space.

030

Pour créer un petit espace baroque, on peut placer une frange de papier vert sur le mur et l'agrémenter d'une autre frange dorée pour parachever le tout, laissant la surface restante en blanc cru.

Um einen kleinen, barocken Raum zu schaffen, kann man einen grünen Papierstreifen auf die Wand kleben und mit einem anderen, goldenen Streifen kombinieren. Die restliche Fläche bleibt naturweiß.

034 This color can also be used to smoothe down the irregular surfaces of walls in rustic buildings, in which case a pale-colored parquet flooring is essential if the feeling of spaciousness is to be kept.

Les murs irréguliers des constructions rustiques deviennent uniformes, une fois peints dans cette couleur. Dans ce cas de figure, il est important de revêtir le sol d'un parquet en bois très clair pour agrandir visuellement les pièces.

Unregelmäßige Wände in rustikalen Häusern wirken in der Farbe Dunkelgrün einheitlich. Der Boden sollte in diesem Fall jedoch mit hellem Holzparkett belegt sein, um den Raum größer wirken zu lassen.

035 A large mirror surrounded by judiciously positioned spotlights and mounted above the washbasin will, together with the chromed metal fixtures, counteract the visually reducing effect of dark-green tiling in bathrooms.

Pour contrecarrer l'effet réducteur des carrelages verts foncés dans les salles de bains, il suffit d'installer un grand miroir, divers spots de lumière dirigés sur le lave-mains, la robinetterie et les accessoires métalliques.

Dunkelgrüne Badezimmerkacheln lassen das Bad kleiner wirken. U diese Wirkung etwas aufzuheben, kann man einen großen Spiegel a hängen und verschiedene Lichtquellen über dem Waschbecken und d Armaturen und anderen Elementen aus Metall anbringen.

036 A few dark-green, Panton plastic chairs around a rustic wooden table v give an informal yet elegant touch to the dining-room.

Pour conférer un air à la fois informel et élégant à une salle à manger, peut avoir recours à des fauteuils vert foncé, disposés autour d'u table en bois rustique.

Um ein Speisezimmer gleichzeitig elegant und unkonventionell wirken lassen, eignen sich Sessel in Dunkelgrün und ein Tisch aus rustikal Holz.

Light Green
Vert clair
Hellgrün

044

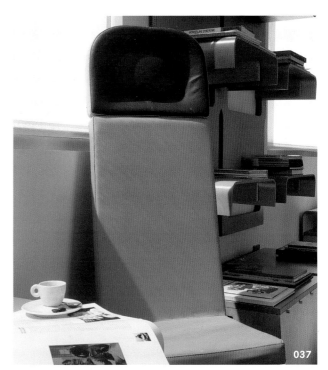

037

037

7 Traditionally associated with industrial environments, brilliant green has become one of the favorite colors of contemporary decoration.

Traditionnellement associé aux environnements industriels, le vert, dans sa gamme plus claire et brillante, est devenu une des couleurs de prédilection de la décoration moderne.

Traditionell wird diese Farbe mit industriellen Umgebungen verbunden. Helles, glänzendes Grün hat sich zu einer der beliebtesten Farben in der modernen Dekoration entwickelt.

8 Furniture with a melamine finish brings informality and youthfulness to kitchens and bathrooms in which chromed metal equipment is predominant.

Les meubles de cette couleur en mélamine ou laqués, apportent une touche juvénile et informelle à la cuisine et la salle de bains, univers où domine l'équipement métallisé.

Möbel aus Melamin oder mit einer grünen Lackierung lassen eine Küche oder ein Bad, in denen Gegenstände aus Metall vorherrschen, jung und unkonventionell wirken.

9 Brilliant green walls combined with white ceilings and moldings help give a contemporary touch to an old house.

Pour donner une touche contemporaine à une maison ancienne, on peut peindre les murs en vert brillant, le plafond et les moulures restant blancs.

Um ein altes Haus moderner wirken zu lassen, kann man die Wände grün und die Decke und das Gesims weiß streichen.

0 For a warm, welcoming atmosphere, a bottle green color combined with yellow lighting is an excellent choice.

Pour créer une ambiance accueillante, le vert bouteille associé à un éclairage jaune est une excellente solution.

Flaschengrün eignet sich ausgezeichnet, um eine einladende Atmosphäre zu schaffen. Ideal in Kombination mit einer gelben Beleuchtung.

041 Ferns in small white pots placed along wide window sills create a kind of mini-greenhouse and provide a refreshing atmosphere.

Les fenêtres profondes, permettent d'aligner des petits pots blancs avec des fougères, créant comme un mini jardin d'hiver, pour doter l'atmosphère de fraîcheur.

An Fenstern mit einer breiten Fensterbank kann man eine Reihe kleiner weißer Blumentöpfe mit Farnen aufstellen. Diese Fenster wirken dann wie kleine Treibhäuser, die dem Raum Frische geben.

042 A green plastic shower curtain gives a contemporary feel to an old, white tiled bathroom.

Un rideau de plastique vert dans la douche apporte une touche de contemporanéité aux salles de bains anciennes habillées de carreaux de céramiques blancs.

Ein grüner Duschvorhang aus Plastik lässt alte Bäder, die mit weißen Kacheln verkleidet sind, modern wirken.

043 Green-painted ironwork on balconies give character and contrast to old apartments in which light tones are predominant.

Les grilles des balcons peintes en vert génèrent un contraste qui donne du caractère aux appartements anciens dominés par les tons clairs.

Grüne Balkongitter bilden einen schönen Kontrast in alten Wohnungen, in denen helle Töne vorherrschen.

040

047

044 Green wallpaper with pastel colored floral patterns evokes the romanti-
cism of 'Chinoiserie' that was so fashionable in the rococo period.
Le papier peint sur fond vert et motifs aux teintes pastel évoque le
romantisme de la « chinoiserie » si en vogue à l'époque rococo.
Tapeten mit grünem Hintergrund und Pflanzenmotiven in Pastelltönen
erinnern an den Romantizismus der „Chinoiserie", die in der Zeit des
Rokoko so beliebt war.

045 Plants with large shiny leaves can be used quite effectively to divide a
room into various areas.
Les plantes vertes à grandes feuilles brillantes peuvent servir de cloison
naturelle au sein d'une même ambiance.
Pflanzen mit großen, glänzenden Blättern können als Raumteiler benutzt
werden.

046 Pale green roller blinds tend to make small windows look larger.
Les stores enroulables vert clair tendent à agrandir visuellement les
petites fenêtres.
Aufrollbare Stores in Hellgrün lassen kleine Fenster optisch größer wirken.

047 Climbing plants and creepers are rather nice for covering interior patio
walls and creating a small oasis of peace in city dwellings.
Les plantes couvrantes et grimpantes sont idéales pour revêtir entièrement les murs des patios intérieurs et créer une petite oasis de verdure
dans les habitations situées en pleine ville.
Kletter- und Schlingpflanzen an den Wänden von Innenhöfen sind eine
wunderschöne Möglichkeit, um eine kleine Oase der Natur mitten in der
Stadt zu schaffen.

048 Acid green walls liven up dark corridors, but only in combination w
pale parquet or ocher-colored tiled floorings.
Les murs peints en vert acidulé aident à animer les couloirs sombr
Dans ce cas de figure, opter de préférence pour un sol en parquet c
ou en carrelage ocre.
Gelbgrüne Wände lassen dunkle Flure lebendig wirken. Dazu passt
ein Boden aus hellem Parkett oder ockerfarbene Fliesen.

039

Blue
Bleu
Blau

051

049 According to the Judeo-Christian tradition, blue is the color of purity and virginity. In Anglo-Saxon countries, however, it is associated with sadness and melancholy, and the type of music that expresses these very feelings is called 'the Blues'.

Dans la tradition judéo-chrétienne, le bleu est la couleur de la pureté et la virginité. Dans les pays anglo-saxons, par contre, il est associé à la tristesse et à la mélancolie. D'où le nom de la musique « blues ».

Der Tradition der Juden und Christen nach ist Blau die Farbe der Reinheit und Jungfräulichkeit. In den angelsächsischen Ländern wird sie jedoch mit Traurigkeit und Melancholie verbunden. Daher auch der Name der Musikrichtung „Blues".

050 This color conveys stillness and tends to be associated with cold climates and objects. Yet, as the color of rivers and oceans, it is inescapably linked to nature.

C'est une couleur apaisante, que l'on associe à des climats et des objets froids. Mais également à l'eau des fleuves et des océans, reflétant son lien inévitable à la nature.

Es handelt sich um eine Farbe, die Ruhe vermittelt und mit kaltem Klima und kalten Objekten in Verbindung gebracht wird. Aber auch mit dem Wasser der Flüsse und Ozeane, denn Blau ist eine Farbe, die eng mit der Natur verbunden ist.

051 Lighter shades of blue are recommended for the walls of small rooms, producing an effect of distance which translates into a feeling of spaciousness.

Appliqué dans ses teintes les plus claires, il est idéal pour peindre l murs des petits espaces, provoquant une impression d'éloignement, o se traduit par une sensation d'amplitude accrue.

Helle Blautöne eignen sich gut für die Wände kleiner Räume, da s diese optisch größer machen.

052 The use of dark blue as the dominant color, however, is not recommer ed as it creates a cold and dark atmosphere.

Par contre, il n'est pas conseillé d'utiliser le bleu sombre en coule dominante, car il engendre un sentiment de froideur et d'obscurité.

Dunkelblau als vorherrschende Farbe ist jedoch nicht empfehlenswe denn es wirkt kalt und dunkel.

053 Painting the ceiling and one of the walls dark blue while leaving the ot ers white will make the height of a room appear much greater.

Les chambres paraîtront plus hautes, en peignant un des murs et le p fond en bleu sombre et le reste en blanc.

Wenn man eine Wand und die Decke eines Raumes dunkelblau streich und die anderen Wände Weiß, wirkt der Raum insgesamt höher.

054 A large mirror with an attractive gilded frame will counteract the effe produced by a dark blue wall and create an elegant corner.

Un grand miroir avec un cadre en or vieilli, casse l'effet sombre d'un m peint en bleu et génère un coin tout en élégance.

Ein großer Spiegel mit einem auffallenden, mit Altgold gestrichene Rahmen hebt die verdunkelnde Wirkung einer blauen Wand etwas a und wirkt sehr elegant.

055

5 Evoking maritime decors, the combination of dark blue and white brings freshness to reduced spaces.

Les ambiances marines, évoquant l'association de cette couleur au blanc, dotent les petits espaces de fraîcheur.

Wenn man Blau mit Weiß kombiniert, schafft man einen frischen Marine-stil für kleinere Räume.

56 White painted wooden floors and blue walls make for a cozy sitting room, with pale natural wood furniture and linen curtains as the perfect finishing touches.

Pour créer un salon accueillant, on peut peindre le parquet en blanc et les murs en bleu. Cette association s'accorde parfaitement aux meubles en bois de teintes naturelles et aux rideaux de lin.

Um ein gemütliches Wohnzimmer zu gestalten, kann man den Holzboden Weiß und die Wände Blau streichen. Diese Kombination passt ausgezeichnet zu Möbeln aus naturfarbenem Holz und Leinengardinen.

57 A small hallway will not require furniture, which would only impede movement, if the wall opposite the front door is decorated with a 70's wallpaper in different shades of blue.

Une petite entrée peut se passer de meubles qui gênent le passage, si on habille le mur face à la porte d'un papier peint de style années soixante-dix, en différents tons de bleu.

In einem kleinen Flur benötigt man keine Möbel, die den Durchgang behindern, wenn man die Wand, die der Tür gegenüberliegt, mit Tapeten im Stile der Sechzigerjahre in verschiedenen Blautönen tapeziert.

058 Blue painted rooms can be given a touch of exoticism with paintings and rugs in reds and oranges.

On peut apporter une touche d'exotisme à des murs peints en bleu, en les associant à des cadres et tapis rouges et oranges.

Räume mit blauen Wänden wirken exotisch, wenn man sie mit Bildern und Teppichen in Rot- und Orangetönen dekoriert.

059 Blue colored plastic or gum decorations applied to window panes filter the sunlight and create a cool atmosphere.

Les gélatines bleues appliquées sur les fenêtres par lesquelles le soleil pénètre à flots, permettent de garder les pièces fraîches.

Blaue Kunststoffbeläge auf Fenstern, durch die viel Sonnenlicht fällt, tragen dazu bei, dass der Raum kühler wirkt.

060 Floors with a brilliant blue resin finish brighten up rooms.

Les sols aux finitions de résine dans un bleu brillant illuminent la pièce.

Fußböden, die mit glänzendem, blauen Kunstharz belegt sind, lassen den Raum hell wirken.

060

050

053

Turquoise
Turquoise
Türkis

072

062

068

067

061 This color owes its name to the blue-green semi-precious stone. Throughout history it has been part of adornment, particularly in ancient cultures such as those of the Egyptians, the Aztecs, the Persians and the Chinese.

Le nom de cette couleur vient de la pierre bleu verdâtre. Tout au long de l'histoire, elle a fait partie de la décoration des civilisations de l'antiquité, que ce soit l'égyptienne, l'aztèque, la perse ou la chinoise.

Der Name dieser Farbe leitet sich von dem gleichnamigen blaugrünen Edelstein ab. Türkise wurden in den alten Kulturen bereits als Schmuckstücke benutzt, z. B. im alten Ägypten, im Aztekenreich, in Persien und in China.

062 It is a peaceful, refreshing and soothing color, suitable for bedrooms and other areas meant for relaxation.

C'est une couleur paisible, rafraîchissante, aux vertus calmantes, propice dans les pièces consacrées au repos.

Es handelt sich um eine sanfte, erfrischende und beruhigende Farbe, die sich ausgezeichnet für Ruhezonen eignet.

063 Associated with the sea, the beach and swimming pools, it goes well with teak garden furniture.

On l'associe à la mer, la plage et les piscines. C'est pour cela qu'elle se marie très bien au bois de teck pour les meubles d'extérieur.

Die Farbe Türkis wird mit dem Meer, dem Strand und mit Schwimmbädern verbunden. Deshalb lässt sie sich gut mit Gartenmöbeln aus Teakholz kombinieren.

064 A complete table setting, crystal vases and jars in this color will give the table a vibrant, contemporary look.

Pour créer une table moderne et joyeuse, choisir une vaisselle complète, verres et cruche en verre, tous de cette même couleur.

Um einen Tisch modern und fröhlich zu decken, kann man ein vollständiges Service, Gläser und Glaskrüge in der gleichen Farbe benutzen.

065 Combined with white, turquoise gives the house a cheerful and refreshing atmosphere.

Sa présence dans des pièces, où elle se mélange aux tons de blanc, forge une atmosphère joyeuse et rafraîchissante.

Wenn man im Raum Türkis mit Weißtönen kombiniert, entsteht eine heitere und erfrischende Atmosphäre.

066 New decorating trends that are bringing back the 'vintage' look include this color for kitchen appliances with rounded edges, and for plastic furniture.

Les tendances actuelles qui exaltent le style vintage utilisent le turquoise pour l'électroménager aux bords arrondis et les meubles en plastique.

Augenblicklich liegt der Vintage-Stil im Trend, bei dem Türkis für Haushaltsgeräte mit abgerundeten Ecken und für Kunststoffmöbel benutzt wird.

067 Turquoise is a contemporary alternative to the traditional baby blue used in children's rooms.

Le turquoise est une alternative moderne au bleu clair, utilisé traditionnellement dans les chambres d'enfants.

065

Türkis ist eine moderne Alternative zu dem Hellblau, das man traditionell in Kinderzimmern benutzt.

068 Its brightness makes turquoise a suitable color for apartments with little natural light as it creates a feeling of spaciousness and depth.

Fort de sa luminosité, le turquoise est une couleur idéale pour les pièces peu éclairées, car elle agrandit visuellement l'espace et déclenche une impression de profondeur accrue.

Da Türkis eine helle Farbe ist, kann man es gut in dunklen Räumen einsetzen. Die Farbe vergrößert den Raum optisch und lässt ihn tiefer wirken.

069 It is also recommended, in combination with white, for floor tile in small bathrooms.

C'est également une couleur à conseiller pour carreler le sol des petites salles de bain en les associant à des mosaïques de verre blanches.

Türkis eignet sich auch gut für den Fußbodenbelag kleiner Bäder in Kombination mit weißen Kacheln.

070 A turquoise rug, about 5' in diameter, is perfect for a transition between the entry hall and living room. The impact of its color will catch visitors' eyes and draw them forward.

Pour délimiter l'entrée intégrée au salon, on peut installer un tapis turquoise de 1,50 m de diamètre. L'impact de la couleur fera converger les regards vers cet espace.

Um einen Eingangsbereich, der in das Wohnzimmer integriert ist, zu begrenzen, kann man einen türkisen Teppich mit einem Durchmesser von 1,50 m auf den Boden legen. Die starke Wirkung der Farbe lenkt die Aufmerksamkeit auf diese Zone.

071 Turquoise colored drapes for windows or sliding glass doors opening o onto a garden offer a pleasant meditation between the interior of th house and the predominant green outside.

Le turquoise des rideaux accrochés aux fenêtres ou aux portes coul santes ouvertes sur le jardin crée une agréable transition, grâce à couleur verte qui prédomine à l'extérieur.

Wenn man türkisfarbene Gardinen an den Fenstern oder Schiebetür aufhängt, die zum Garten liegen, entsteht ein angenehmer Übergang dem Grün im Freien.

072 Accessories such as crystal balls and vases in this color make particul bright spots when catching the natural light. The best place for them of course, near the windows.

Traversés par la lumière du jour, les boules de verre et les vases de co leur brillent énormément. Pour cette raison, il est conseillé de situer c accessoires près des fenêtres.

Türkisfarbene Glaskugeln und Krüge glänzen besonders schön, wer das Tageslicht durch sie dringt. Diese Dekorationselemente sollte man Fensternähe aufstellen.

Violet
Violet
Violett

074

073 Lilac results from the mixing of red and blue, and is associated with the spiritual and emotional. Purple, one of its variations, denotes royalty and magnificence, and is traditionally worn by archbishops.

Le lilas est le résultat du mélange entre le rouge et le bleu, on l'associe aux émotions et à l'esprit. Dans sa nuance tirant vers le violet, il exprime royauté et somptuosité : c'est la couleur des évêques.

Die Farbe Lila entsteht aus der Mischung von Rot und Blau. Sie ruft emotionale und spirituelle Assoziationen hervor. Dunkelviolett wirkt üppig und prachtvoll, und es ist die Farbe der Bischöfe.

074 Very sensitive to natural light, it is best avoided in dark places where it becomes rather lifeless.

Couleur très sensible aux variations de lumière, il est conseillé de ne pas l'appliquer dans les pièces peu éclairées, pour éviter qu'elle ternisse et perde de son éclat.

Es handelt sich um eine Farbe, die sensibel auf Lichtveränderungen reagiert. Man sollte sie nicht in dunklen Räumen verwenden, denn sie würde die Dunkelheit noch verstärken.

075 Being one of nature's basic colors, it can greatly enhance decoration that includes natural wood and fabrics.

Présente dans la nature, c'est une couleur idéale pour mettre en valeur la décoration essentiellement à base de bois et de tissus naturels.

Diese Farbe eignet sich ausgezeichnet für Räume, in denen Holz und natürliche Gewebe vorherrschen, denn man findet sie auch in der Natur sehr oft.

076 Although it can be applied anywhere in the house, its use should b restricted to the dining room or the living room if the whole living spac is not to become somewhat monotonous.

On peut l'utiliser dans n'importe quel espace de la maison, tout en év tant le salon et la salle à manger. Sinon, l'ensemble de l'habitation pre drait un caractère un peu monotone.

Diese Farbe kann in jedem Raum eines Hauses verwendet werden, ab insbesondere eignet sie sich für das Wohn- und das Speisezimmer. Ve wendet man sie in zu vielen Räumen, wirkt die Wohnung oder das Hau monoton.

077 Violet walls and silver-plated accessories give the living room a sobe contemporary look.

Un salon violet, doté d'accessoires en métal argenté, revêt un a moderne et sobre.

Ein Wohnzimmer in Violett mit Dekorationselementen aus silberne Metall wirkt modern und schlicht.

078 Gilded mirrors, lamps and furniture all contribute to a luxurious env ronment.

De leur côté, miroirs, lampes et meubles de bois peints en doré forge une atmosphère luxueuse.

In Kombination mit Spiegeln, Lampen und Holzmöbeln, die mit golden Farbe gestrichen sind, entsteht eine sehr luxuriöse Atmosphäre.

079 Violet is particularly recommended for high ceilings, in combination wi pink or white walls, as it brings the height of the room down.

076

Pour abaisser visuellement les plafonds d'une chambre très haute, il est recommandé de les peindre en violet, et les murs en rose et blanc.
Um Decken in einem hohen Raum optisch niedriger wirken zu lassen, kann man sie violett streichen und die Wände rosa oder weiß.

080 Vinyl paints in this color are not recommended because their brightness is very hard on the eye.
Les peintures vinyliques sont déconseillées pour cette couleur car elles créent des reflets brillants désagréables à l'oeil.
Vinylfarben in Violett sind nicht empfehlenswert: sie glänzen zu stark und irritieren den Betrachter.

081 The most suitable techniques for applying this color involve watering the paint down or creating a marbled effect. Furniture and accessories in natural materials are ideal complements.
La peinture à l'eau et la couleur appliquée à l'éponge sont les techniques préconisées pour que la couleur se marie avec des meubles et accessoires de couleurs naturelles.
Wasserlösliche Farben und die Wischtechnik eignen sich besonders gut für diese Farbe in Kombination mit Möbeln und Dekorationselementen in Naturfarben.

082 Lilac-colored walls can look quite dramatic in sitting rooms that include gray sofas and rugs.
Sur les murs, la couleur lilas rehausse les salons dotés de canapés et tapis gris.
Lilafarbene Wände im Wohnzimmer betonen graue Sofas und Teppiche.

083 The combination of lilac walls and apple-green furniture is one of the most successful recipes for a contemporary look in teenage rooms.
Pour créer une chambre moderne d'adolescents, il suffit de peindre les murs en lilas et de choisir des meubles vert pomme.
Um ein modernes Jugendzimmer zu gestalten, kann man die Wände lila streichen und diese mit apfelgrünen Möbeln kombinieren.

084 Orchids in delicate hues of violet give minimalist environments a touch of elegance.
Dans les ambiances minimalistes, les orchidées, avec leurs délicats tons de lilas, apportent une touche d'élégance.
In minimalistischen Wohnumgebungen sorgen Orchideen mit zarten Violetttönen für Eleganz.

083

Magenta
Magenta
Magenta

086

085 The word 'magenta' comes from Italian. It was inspired by the dark color of all the blood shed in the battle that took place in Magenta on June 4, 1859.
Le mot « magenta » vient de l'italien. Le nom de cette couleur s'inspire de la bataille de Magenta du 4 juin 1859, faisant allusion à la couleur foncée du sang répandu.
Das Wort „Magenta" stammt aus dem Italienischen. Der Name der Farbe ist von der Schlacht bei Magenta am 4. Juni 1859 inspiriert, dabei spielte man auf die dunkle Farbe des vergossenen Blutes an.

086 A single magenta colored neon tube mounted on the main wall of the sitting room is a perfect decorative element for a contemporary, urban touch.
Une seule applique de néon magenta sur le mur principal du salon constitue un élément décoratif de style urbain et moderne.
Durch einen einzigen Auftrag von leuchtendem Magenta auf die Hauptwand im Wohnzimmer entsteht eine urbane und moderne Atmosphäre.

087 It is one of the principal colors employed by the most daring of today's contemporary designers.
C'est une des couleurs les plus utilisées par les designers contemporains.
Es ist eine der Farben, die von modernen Designern am häufigsten verwendet wird.

088 Magenta colored melamine furniture is the best option for an innovative kitchen.
Pour créer une cuisine innovatrice, les meubles en mélamine de cette couleur sont la meilleure alternative.

Um eine innovative Küche zu gestalten, sind Möbel aus Melamin Magenta die beste Lösung.

089 Magenta cushions displayed on a sofa give the living room a touch modernity. A rug of the same color will reinforce this effect.
Les coussins de couleur magenta sur un canapé modernisent le salo
Pour en accentuer l'effet, on peut installer un tapis de la même couleu
Magentafarbene Kissen auf einem grauen Sofa lassen das Wohnzimm
modern wirken. Um diese Wirkung noch zu unterstreichen, kann m
einen Teppich in der gleichen Farbe wählen.

090 The warm, welcoming light generated by magenta-shaded lamps is pe
fect for a hall.
Les lampes aux abat-jour magenta engendrent une lumière très chale
reuse, parfaite pour l'entrée.
Lampen mit einem magentafarbenen Schirm erzeugen ein sehr warm
Licht, das sich gut für den Eingangsbereich eignet.

091 It is an ideal color for delineating a work space under a wood or chrom
steal staircase.
C'est une couleur idéale pour délimiter une zone de travail optimalisa
l'espace sous un escalier de bois ou de métal.
Diese Farbe eignet sich gut, um einen Arbeitsbereich abzugrenzen, f
den man den Raum unter einer Holz- oder Metalltreppe nutzt.

092 The latest decoration trends have made magenta colored acrylic cha
deliers fashionable again. The most creative place for them is in the d
ing room above a natural wood table.

089

Les dernières tendances décoratives remettent au goût du jour les *lustres* de méthacrylique magenta. Les installer dans la salle à manger, suspendus au-dessus d'une table en bois naturel, est une idée innovatrice originale.

Die neusten Trends in der Innenarchitektur haben den Kronleuchter wieder entdeckt; jetzt aus magentafarbenem Metakrylat. Eine innovative Option ist es, diesen über einem Esstisch aus Naturholz im Speisezimmer aufzuhängen.

093 Black deep-pile rugs emphasize the sofas and armchairs in neobaroque surroundings.
Les tapis noirs aux poils longs mettent en valeur les canapés et fauteuils dans les ambiances néo-baroques.
Langhaarige Teppiche und die Farbe Schwarz betonen Sofas und Sessel in einer neobarocken Wohnumgebung.

094 Acrylic paint in this color can be used for small bathrooms, applied to the lower part of the wall as a wainscoting.
Les petites salles de bains peuvent se permettre cette couleur, si elle est appliquée avec une peinture acrylique sur la moitié inférieure du mur.
In kleinen Bädern kann man diese Farbe als Acrylfarbe auf der oberen Hälfte der Wand auftragen.

095 A magenta colored duvet cover in a small bedroom is very effective in creating an illusion of space.
Une housse de couette magenta agrandira une petite chambre à coucher.
Ein kleines Schlafzimmer wirkt durch einen magentafarbenen Bettbezug größer.

096 Painting the wall at the head of the bed magenta is a good alternative to a headboard, which would only take up space in a small bedroom.
Le mur de la tête de lit, peint en magenta, remplacera l'encombrante tête de lit de bois.
Die magentafarben gestrichene Wand am oberen Ende des Bettes kann ein Kopfteil aus Holz ersetzen, das nur Platz beansprucht.

087

Pink
Rose
Rosa

097

099

7 Pink is the result of mixing red with white. Many different shades can be obtained. Add a small amount of yellow to the basic mixture for the brightest pinks or minute quantities of gray for the palest.
Le rose est une couleur qui s'obtient en mélangeant le rouge et le blanc. Il présente une grande variété de nuances qui vont des plus brillantes, avec des pointes de jaune, jusqu'aux roses pâles obtenus en ajoutant des petites doses de blanc.
Rosa ist eine Farbe, die man durch das Mischen von Rot und Weiß erhält. Rosa hat sehr viele Nuancen. Wenn man etwas Gelb hinzugibt, bekommt man ein sehr glänzendes Rosa, und mit einer kleinen Dosis Grau ein Zartrosa.

8 Pink is traditionally associated with femininity. Mixed with brown and bronze colors, however, pink becomes more energetic.
Il est traditionnellement associé à la féminité. Combiné à des tons de marron et bronze, il revêt un caractère plus énergique.
Traditionell wird Rosa mit der Weiblichkeit assoziiert. Wenn man es jedoch mit Braun und Bronze kombiniert, wirkt es energischer.

9 Environments in which pink is the predominant color tend to look romantic or rustic.
Les ambiances dominées par cette couleur prennent souvent un air romantique ou rustique.
Die Räume, in denen diese Farbe vorherrscht, wirken eher romantisch oder auch rustikal.

0 Pink curtains, tablecloths and glassware usually add a touch of fun to the kitchen.

Dans la cuisine, le rose apporte une touche gaie, notamment sur les rideaux, nappes et verreries.
In der Küche wirkt Rosa sehr heiter, vor allem an den Gardinen, Tischdecken und Gläsern.

101 Gentle and serene, pink can help tone down a strong magenta. Painting the walls in both these colors is sure to create a welcoming, intimate atmosphere.
La teinte rose compense, avec sa sérénité et sa douceur, la force du magenta. Avec des murs peints de ces deux couleurs, vous pourrez créer une atmosphère enveloppante, intimiste et très accueillante.
Zartrosa kompensiert mit seiner Gelassenheit und Sanftheit die Kraft der Farbe Magenta. Wenn man die Wände in diesen beiden Farben streicht, schafft man eine betörende, intime und sehr einladende Atmosphäre.

102 Pink and magenta can be used together in living rooms and dining rooms that get a lot of strong natural light or to liven up corridors. They are not recommended for work or study areas.
Où les appliquer : dans les salons et salles à manger où la lumière est abondante et les couloirs pour les égayer. A déconseiller dans les lieux de travail et d'étude.
Die Verwendung von Rosa empfiehlt sich in Wohnzimmern und Speisezimmern mit viel Licht. Flure wirken in der Farbe Rosa heiterer. Die Farbe ist nicht empfehlenswert für Arbeitsräume und Büros.

106

103   Accessories that reflect or filter light, such as silver candlesticks glass-
      bead curtains used for partitioning different spaces, transparent chairs and
      tables of acrylic, are perfect with pink and give it a contemporary look.
      Les accessoires qui laissent passer la lumière ou la reflètent comme les
      chandeliers en argent, les rideaux de mailles de verre pour séparer les
      zones de vie, les sièges et tables transparentes de méthacrylate, sont
      idéals combinés avec le rose pour apporter un air de modernité.
      Dekorationselemente, die lichtdurchlässig sind oder Licht reflektieren,
      z. B. silberne Kandelaber, Gardinen aus Glasperlen als Raumteiler und
      transparente Stühle und Tische aus Metakrylat eignen sich ideal zur
      Kombination mit Rosa. So wirkt der Raum sehr modern.

104   Pink goes particularly well with fresh linen or cotton, especially if those
      fabrics are white, natural or lavender.
      Le rose se marie très bien avec les tissus frais comme le lin et le coton
      essentiellement blanc, mauve ou bleu clair.
      Rosa passt ausgezeichnet zu frischen Stoffen wie Leinen und Baumwol-
      le, vor allem in den Farben Weiß, Mauve und Hellblau.

105   Children's rooms never look dull when different shades of pink are used
      for the walls combined with white furniture and a honey-colored rug.
      Pour éviter une atmosphère terne dans la chambre d'enfants, peindre
      les murs en différents tons de rose et installer des meubles blancs avec
      un tapis de couleur miel.
      Man kann die nichts sagende Dekoration eines Kinderzimmers vermei-
      den, indem man die Wände in verschiedenen Rosatönen streicht und mit
      weißen Möbeln und einem honiggelben Teppich kombiniert.

106   Vinyl wallpapers with abstract motifs in various pinks are perfect for
      ing rooms with retro furniture.
      Les salons aux meubles rétro s'harmonisent parfaitement aux papi
      peints en vinyle dotés de motifs abstraits, déclinés dans différentes te
      tes de rose.
      Wohnzimmer mit Möbeln im Retrostil passen perfekt zu Vinyltapeten
      abstrakten Motiven in verschiedenen Rosatönen.

107   A garden illuminated by pink strips of light at night looks rather elega
      Les guirlandes lumière de cette couleur apportent une touche chi
      l'éclairage nocturne du jardin.
      Lichtgirlanden in Rosa lassen die nächtliche Beleuchtung eines Garte
      sehr schick wirken.

108   For a classical style, use a pink-and-white striped wallpaper on one v
      and either of these colors on the others. Add a black rug for a conte
      porary touch.
      Un mur recouvert de papier à rayures blanches et roses avec le reste
      la chambre dans une des deux couleurs, crée un style classique.
      tapis de couleur noir lui apportera une touche de modernité.
      Eine Wand mit weiß-rosa gestreifter Tapete in Kombination mit
      anderen Wänden in Weiß oder Rosa ist eine klassische Lösung.
      schwarzer Teppich lässt die Atmosphäre dann wieder modern wirken

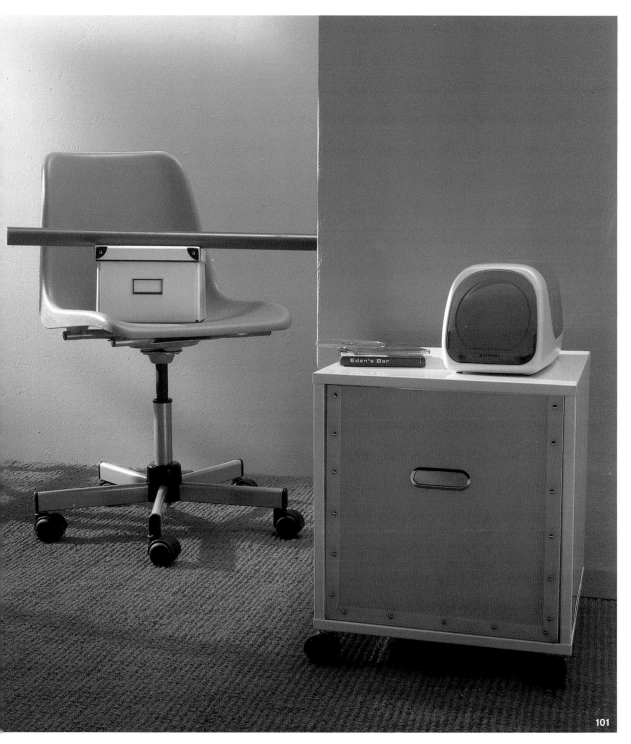

Eden's Bar

Red
Rouge
Rot

114

109 Red is the color of passion. It symbolizes blood, fire, heat, revolution, joy, action, strength and impulse.

Le rouge est la couleur de la passion. Il symbolise le sang, le feu, la chaleur, la révolution, la joie, l'action, la force et l'impulsion.

Rot ist die Farbe der Leidenschaft. Es symbolisiert Blut, Feuer, Hitze, Revolution, Freude, Aktion, Kraft und Schwung.

110 It is one of the prominent colors in Chinese culture. In China it is believed to bring good luck, and gifts of money are traditionally wrapped in red.

C'est un des tons prédominants dans la culture chinoise où il est considéré comme étant la couleur qui porte bonheur. Dans cette société, l'argent est traditionnellement offert dans des paquets rouges.

Rot ist eine der vorherrschenden Farben in der chinesischen Kultur, wo es als die Farbe des Glücks betrachtet wird. In der chinesischen Gesellschaft wird Geld traditionell in roten Paketen verschenkt.

111 Hot and daring, it always delivers a strong impact. This makes it suitable for spaces that are meant to stimulate the mind and stir up emotions, such as places of entertainment.

Chaleureux et audacieux, il saute aux yeux là où il est présent. C'est pourquoi, il est idéal pour les espaces où l'on veut stimuler l'esprit et les sens, comme, à titre d'exemple, dans les chambres destinées aux loisirs.

Es ist eine warme und gewagte Farbe, die überall ins Auge fällt. Deshalb eignet sich Rot gut für Räume, in denen der Geist und die Sinne angeregt werden sollen, z. B. in Räumen, in denen man sich einer Freizeitbeschäftigung widmet.

112 Orange-red gives a feeling of welcome and is therefore ideal for entri

Le rouge corail à la faculté de créer une atmosphère accueillante devient l'option parfaite pour les entrées.

Korallrot ist eine Farbe, die einladend wirkt. Deshalb eignet sie sich a gezeichnet für den Eingangsbereich.

113 In its purest state red can be rather aggressive so it is best used in m eration and kept for decorative details or small spaces.

Utilisé à l'état pur, il peut paraître légèrement violent, c'est pourqu convient de l'appliquer avec modération, sur des détails ou des peti surfaces.

In seinem reinen Zustand kann Rot etwas heftig wirken, deshalb so man diese Farbe mit Zurückhaltung verwenden, z. B. für einzelne De rationselemente oder kleinere Bereiche.

114 Red is generally used for creating specific effects, such as draw attention to an architectural element (a staircase or column) or to a s gle wall.

En général, le rouge est employé pour créer des effets bien défir comme par exemple, attirer l'attention sur un élément architectu (escaliers ou colonnes) ou un mur unique.

Im Allgemeinen wird Rot dazu benutzt, eine ganz bestimmte Wirkung erzielen, zum Beispiel die Aufmerksamkeit auf ein architektonisches E ment (Treppen oder Säulen) oder eine einzigartige Wand zu lenken.

115 If applied to walls with large openings, red becomes attractive witho being overpowering as the surface it covers is not as great.

113

Il est idéal à appliquer sur les murs aux grandes ouvertures. Sur une petite superficie, il attire le regard sans trop charger l'atmosphère.

Es eignet sich ausgezeichnet für Wände mit großen Fensterflächen. Da die rote Oberfläche dann nicht allzu groß ist, wirkt die Umgebung nicht überladen und man erzielt ein sehr schönes Ergebnis.

6 It can also be used for background walls in contrast with another color in spaces that include arches or galleries.

Il peut également être utilisé sur les murs de fond dans les espaces avec arcades ou galeries, dotés d'une couleur contrastée.

Rot eignet sich auch für die hinteren Wände in Räumen mit Bögen oder Galerien, die in einer Kontrastfarbe gestrichen sind.

7 Combined with solid-pine furniture, orange red is ideal for converting rustic environments into contemporary spaces.

Le rouge corail est parfait pour transformer les ambiances à l'air rustique, agrémentées de meubles en pin dans les espaces modernes.

Korallrot eignet sich ausgezeichnet, um rustikale Einrichtungen mit Möbeln aus Kiefernholz in eine moderne Wohnumgebung umzugestalten.

8 White painted doors and door frames help tone it down and create a very pleasing contrast. Classic furniture and large, brightly colored rugs are the perfect addition.

Pour diminuer son intensité, il est conseillé de peindre en blanc les portes et cadres, créant ainsi un contraste très intéressant. Les meubles classiques et les grands tapis de couleurs vives se marient parfaitement à cette couleur si chaude.

Um die Intensität der Farbe Rot etwas abzuschwächen, kann man die Türen und Fensterrahmen weiß streichen. So entsteht ein schöner Kontrast. Klassische Möbel und große Teppiche in kräftigen Farben passen gut zu der warmen Farbe Rot.

119 Traditionally associated with rustic environments, russet red also works very well in urban residences when combined with grays and intense blues.

Traditionnellement associé au rustique, le rouge brique est parfait pour les ambiances urbaines, assorti de gris et bleus intenses.

Traditionell assoziiert man Ziegelrot mit einer rustikalen Umgebung, aber die Farbe eignet sich auch für urbane Wohnungen, wenn man sie mit Grautönen und intensivem Blau kombiniert.

120 The sophistication and strong personality of crimson red and burgundy make them ideal for sitting rooms, bedrooms and work spaces.

Le rouge anglais ou lie de vin se démarque par son élégance et sa personnalité. Il est idéal pour les salons, chambres à coucher et espaces de travail.

Englischrot und Weinrot wirken sehr elegant und persönlich und eignen sich deshalb ausgezeichnet für Wohnzimmer, Schlafzimmer und Arbeitsräume.

115

111

112

120

Orange
Orange
Orange

129

125

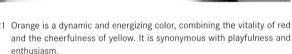

123

128

1 Orange is a dynamic and energizing color, combining the vitality of red and the cheerfulness of yellow. It is synonymous with playfulness and enthusiasm.

L'orange est une couleur énergique et stimulante. Il conjugue la vitalité du rouge et l'optimisme du jaune. On l'associe à la gaieté et l'enthousiasme.

Orange ist eine kraftvolle und anregende Farbe. Es kombiniert die Vitalität von Rot mit der Freude von Gelb. Diese Farbe wird mit Heiterkeit und Begeisterung assoziiert.

2 Human perception of this color is thought to increase oxygen to the brain. Its capacity for stimulating and sharpening mental activity makes it especially suitable for work and entertainment areas.

La perception de cette couleur crée un plus grand apport d'oxygène au cerveau : avec son effet revigorant et stimulant de l'activité mentale, il est parfait pour les espaces de travail et de loisirs.

Die Wahrnehmung dieser Farbe führt zu einer größeren Sauerstoffzufuhr im Hirn, so dass sie stärkend und anregend auf die Gehirnaktivitäten wirkt. Deshalb eignet sich Orange ausgezeichnet für Arbeits- und Trainingsräume.

3 Orange promotes geniality and brightens up even the darkest spaces.

L'orange crée un sentiment accueillant et confère luminosité aux pièces plus sombres.

Orange wirkt freundlich und macht dunklere Räume hell.

4 It is suitable for cold walls or walls with very little insulation as it generates a sensation of warmth.

Il est idéal pour les murs plus froids, ceux qui sont les moins ensoleillés, parce qu'il donne une sensation de chaleur.

Die Farbe eignet sich gut für kältere Wände, auf die weniger Sonnenlicht fällt, denn sie wirkt warm.

125 This color is often present in the decoration of contemporary kitchens because, quite apart from the vitality it brings, it is also associated with food.

C'est une couleur que l'on utilise souvent pour la décoration des cuisines modernes, car, outre la vitalité qu'elle dégage, on l'associe à l'alimentation.

Es handelt sich um eine Farbe, die häufig in modernen Küchen anzutreffen ist, denn außer mit Vitalität wird sie auch mit Lebensmitteln assoziiert.

126 Orange-lacquered kitchen or bathroom furniture impart the perfect contemporary touch.

Des meubles laqués dans cette couleur pour la cuisine ou la salle de bains donneront une touche définitivement contemporaine.

Orange lackierte Möbel für die Küche und das Bad wirken sehr modern.

127 One of the most characteristic colors of the 1970s, it is vital for recreating retro ambiences.

Pour avoir été une des couleurs caractéristiques des années soixante-dix, l'orange est particulièrement indiqué pour créer des ambiances rétro.

Da Orange eine der typischen Farben der Siebzigerjahre war, eignet es sich gut für Wohnumgebungen im Retrostil, insbesondere in Kombination mit Türkis.

127

128 Shiny orange leather or plastic furniture with rounded edges is just the right complement for a 'vintage' look.

Pour compléter un style *vintage*, on peut recourir à l'orange pour les meubles brillants, aux formes incurvées, réalisés en peau, cuir ou plastique.

Für den Vintage-Stil kann man Orange für glänzende Möbel mit gekrümmten Formen aus Leder, Kunstleder oder Kunststoff benutzen.

129 Current decoration trends also include orange and its various tints in the list of suitable colors for minimalist environments with chocolate-brown or black furniture.

La tendance actuelle accepte aussi cette gamme de couleur dans les ambiances minimalistes ou domine le mobilier de couleurs sombres comme le chocolat et le noir.

Augenblicklich liegt es im Trend, diese Farbe auch für minimalistische Umgebungen zu benutzen, in denen Möbel in dunklen Farben, wie Schokoladenbraun oder Schwarz, vorherrschen.

130 Combined with magenta and red, it is reminiscent of Asian-style surroundings and can be used together with white paper lampshades and classic rectangular furniture for exotic minimalism.

Associé au magenta et au rouge, il crée des ambiances d'inspiration asiatique. Dans ces décors, les lampes blanches en papier et le mobilier aux lignes droites engendrent une sorte de minimalisme exotique.

In Kombination mit Magenta und Rot wirkt die Wohnumgebung asiatisch. In einer so gestalteten Wohnung lassen weiße Papierlampen und geradlinige Möbel einen minimalistischen und gleichzeitig exotischen Stil entstehen.

131 The contrast between orange walls and white furniture makes fo fresh, youthful environment.

Les ambiances fraîches et juvéniles utilisent l'orange en contraste a des murs et meubles blancs.

Für frische und junge Wohnumgebungen eignet sich Orange als Kont zu weißen Wänden und Möbeln.

132 Due to the intensity of this color, orange painted rooms should no overloaded with pictures and accessories.

Dû à son intensité, il est conseillé de ne pas charger les pièces orar de cadre ou accessoires.

Aufgrund seiner Intensität sollte man orangefarbene Räume nicht Bildern und Dekorationselementen überladen.

132

Brown
Marron
Braun

135

133 Brown is masculine, severe and comfortable. It is reminiscent of autumn and induces a feeling of gravity and balance.
Le marron est masculin, sévère et confortable. Sa présence évoque l'atmosphère automnale et crée une impression de gravité et d'équilibre.
Braun ist eine männliche, strenge und gemütliche Farbe. Braun schafft eine herbstliche Atmosphäre und wirkt schwer und ausgeglichen.

134 As part of the group of colors present in nature, it acts as a transition between outdoor and indoor spaces.
Intégré au groupe des couleurs de la nature, il fait la transition entre les espaces à l'air libre et les intérieurs.
Da Braun zu den Naturfarben gehört, eignet es sich gut für den Übergang zwischen Räumen im Freien und geschlossenen Räumen.

135 Its darkest shades work in the same way as black, making it possible to combine furnishings in many different ways.
Dans sa gamme plus foncée, il fonctionne comme le noir, dans le sens où, sur le mobilier, il accepte une infinie variété de combinaisons.
In seiner tiefsten Tönung funktioniert es wie Schwarz, d. h. auch braune Möbel lassen sich auf viele verschiedene Weisen kombinieren.

136 A brown-painted room tends to look a lot smaller. Alternating brown with pink will achieve the opposite result while creating an elegant composition in the process.
Une chambre peinte uniquement en marron semblera très petite. Une des façons de l'agrandir visuellement est de l'alterner avec le rose, créant ainsi une composition élégante.

Wenn man einen Raum ausschließlich braun streicht, wirkt er sehr kl
Eine Option, um ihn visuell zu vergrößern, ist es, Braun mit Rosa ab
wechseln. So entsteht eine elegante Komposition.

137 The oxide-paint technique gives this color a gray silvery shine *
makes it come to life.
La technique de peinture à l'oxyde confère à cette couleur des scint
ments gris et argent qui l'illuminent.
Wenn man Oxidfarbe verwendet, glänzt Braun in Grau- und Silbertö
und wirkt so leuchtender.

138 A brown rug provides a contemporary counterpoint to a blue sofa.
Un tapis marron s'offre en contrepoint moderne aux canapés tapis
de bleu.
Ein brauner Teppich dient als moderner Kontrapunkt zu blau bezoge
Sofas.

139 Bookshelves can be emphasized by painting the background wall in color.
Pour rehausser une étagère contenant des livres, il suffit de peindr
mur du fond de cette couleur.
Um ein Bücherregal optisch hervorzuheben, kann man die Wand im
tergrund braun streichen.

140 Flooring of glass mosaic tiles in shades of brown or beige enlarges b
rooms of rather limited proportions.

134

143

Appliquer des mosaïques de verre de couleur marron ou beige dans une salle de bains aux proportions réduites, est une façon judicieuse de l'agrandir visuellement.

Ein kleines Bad wirkt größer, wenn man die Wände mit Mosaikkacheln aus Glaskeramik in Braun oder Beige kachelt.

141 A rectangular room will appear more spacious if the narrowest walls are painted beige and the others dark brown.

Pour agrandir visuellement une pièce rectangulaire, on peut peindre les murs plus étroits en beige et les autres dans une couleur sombre comme le marron chocolat.

Um einen rechteckigen Raum optisch zu vergrößern, kann man die schmaleren Wände Beige und die übrigen in einer dunklen Farbe wie Schokoladenbraun streichen.

142 Rooms clad in brown marble can be given a contemporary look with powerful spotlights mounted on the ceiling.

Les chambres revêtues de dalles de marbre marron acquièrent un air contemporain, si on lui ajoute un éclairage puissant dissimulé dans les joints du plafond.

Räume, die mit Marmorplatten verkleidet sind, wirken mit einer kräftigen Beleuchtung, die die Deckenfugen verbirgt, sehr modern.

143 Brown is useful for visually enlarging a room that is predominantly finished with woodwork.

Cette couleur permet d'agrandir visuellement les murs d'une chambre dans laquelle le bois prédomine.

Die Farbe Braun eignet sich ausgezeichnet, um die Wände eines Zimmers mit Holzrahmen optisch zu vergrößern.

144 One way of creating a feeling of spaciousness in kitchens with dark wood cupboards is by painting the walls orange red and installing a matt metal work surface.

Pour donner un sentiment d'espace aux cuisines dotées d'armoires aux tons de bois foncé, il est conseillé de peindre les murs en rouge corail et d'installer les plans de travail en métal mat.

Um eine Küche mit dunklen Holzmöbeln größer wirken zu lassen, kann man die Wände Korallrot streichen und Arbeitsplatten aus opakem Metall montieren.

140

Black
Noir
Schwarz

149

145 Black can be defined as the absence of any visible light or as the combination of all pigments. Although it tends to draw attention, its use should be restricted to well-lit spaces.

La couleur noire peut se définir comme une absence de lumière visible ou comme le mélange de tous les pigments. Comme elle attire beaucoup le regard, il est recommandé de la restreindre aux espaces très bien éclairés.

Die Farbe Schwarz kann man als die Abwesenheit des sichtbaren Lichtes oder die Kombination aller Pigmente definieren. Auch wenn Schwarz stets die Aufmerksamkeit auf sich zieht, sollte man es nur in gut beleuchteten Räumen benutzen.

146 It is one of the star colors of contemporary interior design. Its strong presence has now reached spaces which, traditionally, have tended to be more personal, such as bathrooms and kitchens.

C'est une des couleurs phares de l'architecture d'intérieur contemporaine. Elle est devenue protagoniste des espaces où elle était traditionnellement bannie, à l'instar des salles de bains et cuisines.

Es ist eine der beliebtesten Farben in der modernen Raumgestaltung. Schwarz spielt mittlerweile auch eine wichtige Rolle in Räumen wie Bädern oder Küchen, aus denen es früher verbannt war.

147 Today black washbasins, toilets, bathtubs and other fittings co-exist happily in small bathrooms with light-colored or unglazed tile wall surfaces.

Lavabos, sanitaires et baignoires en céramique noire cohabitent aujourd'hui harmonieusement dans les petites salles de bains, si les murs restent dans des tons clairs ou sont dotés de revêtements opaques.

Schwarze Handwaschbecken, Toiletten und Badewannen wirken auch kleinen Bädern harmonisch, wenn man sie mit hellen Wänden oder o ken Wandverkleidungen kombiniert.

148 It sets off the geometrical lines of modern residences, as well as slid doors, partitioning walls and staircases.

C'est une couleur idéale pour rehausser les lignes géométriques c habitations modernes et mettre en valeur les portes coulissantes in rieures, murs de partition et escaliers.

Die Farbe Schwarz eignet sich ausgezeichnet, um geometrische Lin in modernen Wohnungen hervorzuheben und um Schiebetüren zwisch Räumen, Trennwände und Treppen auffallend zu gestalten.

149 Black elements such as floor lamps with fabric shades, curtains, rugs a decorative accessories are often included in Neobaroque environment

Les ambiances de style néo-baroque utilisent cette couleur pour les la pes avec abat-jour en tissu, rideaux, tapis et accessoires de décoratio

In neobarocken Wohnumgebungen wird diese Farbe für Stehlampen Stoffschirmen, Gardinen, Teppiche und Dekorationsgegenstände benu

150 A decoration scheme in which black is the dominant color in a black-a white combination creates a harmonious effect throughout the house.

La décoration où le noir domine, associé au blanc, crée un effet harr nieux valable dans toutes les pièces de la maison.

Die Kombination von Schwarz und Weiß wirkt harmonisch und eig sich für alle Räume eines Hauses.

146

150

151 Wallpapers with black geometrical patterns on a white background promote concentration.
Les papiers peints aux motifs géométriques noirs sur fond blanc contribuent à attirer le regard.
Tapeten mit geometrischen Motiven in Schwarz auf weißem Hintergrund lenken die Aufmerksamkeit auf sich.

52 If black painted or lacquered wood furniture is chosen, all the pieces should be the same color.
Lorsque les meubles sont en bois peint ou laqué noir, il faut que toutes les pièces gardent cette même couleur.
Wenn die Möbel aus schwarzem Holz oder schwarz lackiert sind, sollten sie alle den gleichen Farbton haben.

53 Black tile and black parquet flooring give character to minimalist houses.
Les sols noirs, carrelage ou parquet, dotent les maisons minimalistes de personnalité.
Böden mit schwarzen Fliesen oder schwarzem Parkett verleihen minimalistisch gestalteten Räumen mehr Persönlichkeit.

54 Metal is one of the design elements most commonly used to enhance black.
Pour faire ressortir le noir, le métal est un des éléments les plus employés en décoration.
Um die Farbe Schwarz zu betonen, wird sehr häufig Metall als Material benutzt.

155 A contemporary, 'state-of-the-art' table requires opaque black china, glassware and napkins.
Une table tendance s'affiche avec une vaisselle opaque noire, des verres et serviettes de la même couleur.
Für einen modern gedeckten Tisch benutzt man schwarzes, opakes Geschirr und gleichfarbige Gläser und Servietten.

156 Black-glass partitions ensure privacy in en suite bathrooms.
Les fermetures intérieures en verre de couleur noire préservent l'intimité des salles de bains intégrées à la chambre à coucher.
Innere Raumteiler aus schwarzem Glas schaffen Privatsphäre in Badezimmern, die ins Schlafzimmer integriert sind.

154

White
Blanc
Weiß

159

165

167

162

57 White is synonymous with maximum brightness. It can, in its purest state, prove far too bright for the eye.
Le blanc apporte le maximum de luminosité. C'est une couleur raffinée et pure. A l'état pur, cette grande clarté semble, parfois, agresser le regard.
Weiß ist die hellste Farbe. Diese Farbe verfeinert und reinigt. Im Reinzustand kann ihre Helligkeit manchmal aggressiv auf das Auge wirken.

58 One of its best features is versatility, as it can be part of any decorative scheme.
Une des caractéristiques les plus appréciées de cette couleur, c'est la possibilité de l'intégrer dans presque toutes les propositions de décoration.
Eine ihrer besten Eigenschaften ist die Vielseitigkeit. Dadurch kann sie zum Teil jeder Einrichtung werden.

59 Depending on its composition, white can boast a great variety of shades. The warmest ones contain small quantities of yellow and the coldest include light touches of blue.
Le blanc contient une grande variété de gammes selon sa composition, depuis les plus chaudes — en mélangeant des petites quantités de jaune — jusqu'aux plus froides aux nuances bleutées.
Je nach Mischungsverhältnis, kann Weiß durch eine Vielzahl von Schattierungen glänzen. Die Mischung mit Gelb ergibt ein warmes Weiß, mit Blautönen eher eine kalte Farbe.

60 Ivory, for instance, is associated with comfort as it is a soothing color for tired eyes. It is also suitable for any kind of surrounding.
Dans sa nuance ivoire, c'est une couleur qui s'associe au confort, car elle repose le regard. Elle s'adapte ainsi à n'importe quel type d'ambiance.
Elfenbein ist eine Farbe, die sehr angenehm und entspannend für das Auge ist. Deshalb eignet sich diese Farbe für alle Räume.

161 The light given off by white makes it one of the best options for darker rooms.
La lumière que le blanc dégage, en fait une des meilleures options pour les chambres plus sombres.
Da Weiß das Licht reflektiert, eignet es sich ausgezeichnet für dunklere Räume.

162 It is ideal for making the structural parts of a house, such as wooden beams or columns, appear lighter.
Elle est idéale pour alléger les éléments structuraux de la maison, à l'instar de poutres et piliers de bois ou métal.
Mit der Farbe Weiß kann man die Strukturelemente eines Hauses wie Holzbalken, Metallträger und Säulen leichter wirken lassen.

163 In rooms where alternate colors are to be applied, the wall facing the window should always be painted white so as to reflect the light onto the other surfaces.
Dans les chambres où les murs déclinent une alternance de couleur, il est conseillé que le mur blanc soit face à la fenêtre pour qu'il renvoie la lumière dans le reste de la pièce.
In Räumen, deren Wände in verschiedenen Farben gestrichen sind, sollte die Wand, die dem Fenster gegenüberliegt, weiß sein, damit sie das Licht auf die anderen Wände reflektiert.

160

164 White baseboards with a lacquered finish can give plain white walls a more attractive look.
Pour rendre les murs blancs plus attrayants, il suffit d'appliquer un socle avec des lames laquées de la même couleur.
Um weiße Wände ästhetisch zu verschönern, kann man einen Sockel aus weiß lackierten Streifen schaffen.

165 To avoid the antiseptic aspect of white-painted environments and alleviate their uniformity, it is important to choose bold, colorful decorative items or ones with a variety of textures.
Pour éviter l'aspect aseptisé des ambiances peintes en blanc, il suffit de choisir un détail attrayant ou personnel, légèrement coloré ou une variété de textures qui brise l'uniformité.
Durchgehend weiße Räume wirken leicht steril, deshalb sollte man sie mit einem auffallenden oder persönlichen Element dekorieren, einem bunten Gegenstand oder mit verschiedenen Texturen, die diese Einheitlichkeit unterbrechen.

166 One way of enlarging small windows is to paint a white border around the window frame.
Une façon d'agrandir visuellement les petites fenêtres, est de cerner l'encadrement d'un filet blanc.
Eine Methode, um kleine Fenster optisch zu vergrößern, besteht darin, den Fensterrahmen weiß zu umranden.

167 A coat of linen-white paint gives old furniture a contemporary aspect.
Les vieux meubles de bois peints en blanc, couleur lin, prennent de allures modernes.
Alte Holzmöbel, die man in Naturweiß streicht, wirken modern.

168 Wide, ivory painted floorboards help create a sense of spaciousness.
Les sols faits de longues lattes de bois décapées et peintes en blar ivoire agrandissent l'espace.
Böden mit langen Holzleisten aus abgebeiztem, eierschalenfarben gest chenem Holz lassen den Raum größer wirken.

Gray
Gris
Grau

179

169 Gray can be obtained by mixing black and white in different proportions. Depending on the amount of light, the human eye can interpret it as different color.

Le gris s'obtient en mélangeant différentes quantités de blanc et noir. Selon la quantité de lumière, l'oeil humain peut l'interpréter comme une autre couleur.

Grau entsteht durch das Vermischen verschiedener Anteile an Weiß und Schwarz. Je nach Lichtmenge kann das menschliche Auge Grau als eine andere Farbe interpretieren.

170 It is not a color that provokes strong emotions. Quite the reverse, it creates the kind of atmosphere that encourages meditation and imagination. C'est une couleur qui ne déclenche pas d'émotions fortes. Elle crée des ambiances favorables à la réflexion et à l'imagination.

Die Farbe Grau ruft keine starken Gefühlsbewegungen hervor. Sie schafft Wohnumgebungen, die meditativ wirken und die Phantasie anregen.

171 Gray epoxy-resin based tiles can be combined successfully with all colors and, when used throughout the house, enlarge space because of the sense of continuity they generate.

Les carrelages à base d'époxy grise se marient bien à toutes les couleurs et agrandissent visuellement l'espace, s'ils sont utilisés dans toute la maison, générant ainsi un sentiment de fluidité.

Graue Fußbodenbeläge auf Epoxydbasis passen zu allen Farben und lassen, falls man sie in der ganzen Wohnung oder im ganzen Haus verwendet, den Raum größer wirken, denn es entsteht eine räumliche Kontinuität.

172 The peaceful quality of pebble gray is due to the very small amount black in its composition and makes it perfect for any space in the hous from the kitchen to the bedroom.

Le gris pierre, qui contient peu de noir, est de par son caractère paisib idéal pour tout espace de vie, de la cuisine à la chambre à coucher.

Steingrau, mit einem kleinen Anteil an Schwarz, wirkt sehr beruhige und eignet sich deshalb für jeden Raum im Haus, angefangen bei d Küche bis hin zum Schlafzimmer.

173 The lightest shade of gray is suitable for areas that do not enjoy a lot light as it brightens them up.

Dans sa version plus claire, le gris est approprié pour des zones p lumineuses parce qu'il génère de la clarté.

Die Farbe Hellgrau eignet sich für dunklere Räume, weil sie Helligk schafft.

174 Lead gray, on the other hand, should only be used for large, lig drenched rooms as its intensity tends to reduce spaces.

Le gris plomb, quant à lui, ne peut être appliqué que dans les grand chambres très lumineuses, car son intensité tend à réduire visuelleme les pièces.

Bleigrau jedoch sollte man nur in hellen und großen Räumen verwend Diese intensive Farbe lässt den Raum optisch kleiner wirken.

175 Pebble gray is perfect for highlighting architectural details such as st cases, fireplaces or galleries in small places.

172

Le gris pierre est parfait pour faire ressortir des détails architecturaux dans les petits univers, à l'instar d'un escalier, une cheminée ou une galerie.
Steingrau ist die perfekte Farbe, um architektonische Details wie Treppen, einen Kamin oder eine Galerie in kleinen Räumen hervorzuheben.

6   The elegance of gray can be enhanced by steel or white-metal complements and furniture with simple, straight lines.
Pour renforcer l'élégance du gris, il est conseillé d'utiliser des accessoires en acier ou de couleur argent et un mobilier aux lignes droites.
Um die Eleganz der Farbe Grau noch zu unterstreichen, eignen sich Elemente aus Stahl oder in Silber und Möbel mit geraden Linien

7   Walls clad in gray stone give environments a contemporary feel.
Les murs revêtus de pierre de cette couleur créent des ambiances contemporaines.
Wände, die mit grauem Stein verkleidet sind, machen den Raum sehr modern.

8   Contrasting plain gray concrete and warm-colored furniture is one of the design schemes most in vogue.
Le béton apparent – de couleur grise – souvent mis en contraste avec un mobilier aux tons chauds, est une des matières les plus utilisées dans la décoration actuelle.
Unverputzter, grauer Beton, der oft mit Möbeln in warmen Farben kombiniert wird, ist ein Trend, der in der heutigen Raumgestaltung sehr häufig zu finden ist.

179   Soft, pale fabrics are the kind that best combine with this color.
Les tissus aux textures douces et aux tons clairs sont ceux qui s'harmonisent le mieux avec cette couleur.
Stoffe mit einer weichen Textur und in hellen Farben passen am besten zu Grau.

180   Lead gray upholstery makes for pure and elegant surroundings, whether it is combined with delicate earth-color tints or more vibrant ones, such as reds or oranges.
Les tapis de couleur gris plomb créent des ambiances limpides et élégantes, surtout en association avec des tons clairs ou couleur terre ou avec d'autres plus vibrants, comme le rouge ou l'orange.
Durch Bezüge in Bleigrau entstehen klare und elegante Räume, egal, ob man sie mit hellen, erdfarbenen oder mit kräftigeren Farben wie z. B. Rot oder Orange kombiniert.

176

178

Gold
Or
Gold

182

181 As a variation of yellow, this color creates the visual sensation normally associated with the brilliance of metallic gold.

Nuance de jaune, cette couleur crée une impression visuelle généralement liée à l'éclat métallique de l'or.

Gold ist eine Nuance der Farbe Gelb. Diese Farbe wird mit dem Glanz des Edelmetalls Gold assoziiert.

182 Gold includes a range of warm colors that often bring on a feeling of joy and liveliness. However, it can also create a cheerless, stodgy environment depending on the kind of elements it is combined with.

L'or intègre la gamme des couleurs chaudes et, par conséquent éveille un sentiment de joie et vivacité. Toutefois, selon l'association réalisée, il peut créer une ambiance plus sombre et traditionnelle.

Gold ist eine warme Farbe und wirkt somit heiter und lebendig. Je nachdem, wie man diese Farbe kombiniert, kann auch eine strengere und traditionellere Atmosphäre entstehen.

183 The latest decoration trends have brought this color back into fashion and use it in metallic accessories and glass mosaic tiles.

En décoration, les dernières tendances modernes ont remis cette couleur au goût du jour, en l'utilisant dans les accessoires métallisés et dans les mosaïques de verre.

Die modernen Trends in der heutigen Raumgestaltung haben diese Farbe neu entdeckt, und man findet sie an metallischen Dekorationselementen und Glasmosaiken.

184 A dark bathroom gains in luminosity if gold-colored tiles are applied to one of its walls.

Les salles de bains sombres gagnent en luminosité, si on applique ⊙ mosaïques dorées sur un mur.

Dunkle Bäder wirken heller, wenn man die Wände mit goldenen Mosa kacheln verkleidet.

185 It is also the best ally of neobaroque environments.

C'est également le meilleur allié des tendances néo-baroques.

Ebenso gut passt Gold in neobarocke Einrichtungen.

186 Together with red and crimson, it is reminiscent of tribal or exotic mospheres.

Associé au rouge ou grenat, il tend à engendrer des ambiances d'ins ration ethnique ou exotique.

In Kombination mit Rot- und Granatrottönen entstehen ethnisch gepr te und exotische Räume.

187 A gold silky bedspread can enhance the bedroom. In this case, on single range of earth colors or grays should be used in the decoratio

Un couvre-lit en soie de cette couleur rehausse les chambres à couch Dans ce cas, il est important d'employer dans la chambre une se gamme de couleurs terre ou grise.

Eine seidene Tagesdecke in dieser Farbe ist ein Glanzlicht für das Sch zimmer. Jedoch ist es in diesem Fall wichtig, dass in dem Raum nur e einzige Serie von Erd- oder Grautönen benutzt wurde.

188 Installing gold-colored taps and work surface areas in kitchens wh steel fixtures tend to be the dominant element can offer a chic, eleg solution.

183

Une solution *chic* et élégante pour les cuisines où l'acier est la vedette, est d'installer des robinetteries et un plan de travail en métal doré.

Eine schicke und elegante Lösung für Küchen, in denen Stahl vorherrscht, ist es, Armaturen und eine Arbeitsplatte in metallischem Gold zu installieren.

9   The renowned designer Jaime Hayón recommends a gold-colored external finish for washbasins.

L'éminent designer Jaime Hayón propose, pour les salles de bains, des lavabos aux finitions extérieures de couleur dorée.

Der bekannte Raumgestalter Jaime Hayón schlägt goldene Waschbecken für Badezimmer vor.

0   It is the traditional color of statues and other representations of the Buddha. Oriental decors can combine gold with an ocher tone and indirect lighting.

C'est la couleur utilisée pour représenter Bouddha. Les ambiances de style zen peuvent conjuguer ce ton avec l'ocre et un éclairage indirect.

In dieser Farbe wird Buddha dargestellt. In Wohnumgebungen im Zen-Stil kann man die Farbe Gold mit Ocker und indirekter Beleuchtung kombinieren.

1   A favorite with contemporary designers: Philippe Starck designed the 'Lago' chair, of rigid polyurethane and a gold-colored lacquer finish, for Driade. The Campana brothers used gold for the 'Brasilia' dining table, created for Edra.

C'est une des couleurs de prédilection des designers contemporains. Philippe Starck a conçu pour Driade le fauteuil « Lago », fabriqué en polyuréthanne rigide, laqué d'or. Les frères Campana l'ont utilisé pour la table de salle à manger « Brasilia », créée pour Edra.

Gold ist eine der Lieblingsfarben der zeitgenössischen Designer. Philippe Starck entwarf für Driade den Stuhl „Lago" aus festem Polyurethan in goldener Lackierung. Die Gebrüder Campana benutzten den Esszimmertisch „Brasilia" von Edra.

192 The pure lines of gold-plated cutlery, a rediscovered classic, combine perfectly with a pastel-colored china range.

La ménagère dorée, aux formes pures, est un classique revisité qui se marie à merveille avec la vaisselle aux tons pastel.

Goldenes Besteck mit reinen Linien ist ein klassisches Element für den Tisch, das man perfekt mit pastellfarbenem Geschirr kombinieren kann.

181

Silver
Argent
Silber

193

201

204

202

3 A silver finish makes an enormous visual impact and, far from appearing too flashy, has practically become a must in modern interiors.
Les finitions métallisées en argent produisent un énorme impact visuel et, loin de paraître osées, elles sont aujourd'hui une option quasi incontournable dans les intérieurs modernes.
Metallische silberne Flächen fallen sehr stark ins Auge. Heute empfindet man diese nicht mehr als gewagt, sondern sie sind ein häufig anzutreffendes Mittel in der modernen Raumgestaltung.

4 The new basalt, sandstone and slate floor coverings have a metallic aspect which gives their surfaces a silvery finish.
Les nouveaux revêtements en pierre basaltique, grès et ardoise ont un aspect métallique qui donne aux surfaces un fini couleur argent.
Die neuen Verkleidungen aus Basaltgestein, Sandstein oder Schiefer haben ein metallisches Aussehen, das die Flächen silbern glänzen lässt.

5 Leather poufs with steel trimmings are a good option for catching the light and livening up a sitting room dominated by grays, browns and blues.
Les poufs de peau aux finitions d'acier sont un choix judicieux pour intégrer des touches de lumière dans un salon dominé par les gris, marrons et bleus.
Puffs aus Leder, in Kombination mit Stahl, bringen etwas Licht in ein Wohnzimmer, in dem Grau-, Braun- und Blautöne dominieren.

6 Titanium tiles on floors and walls make small bathrooms appear more spacious.
Les dalles de titane, utilisées pour revêtir sols et murs, agrandissent visuellement les petites salles de bains.

Kacheln aus Titan, mit denen Böden und Wände gekachelt werden, lassen kleine Bäder visuell größer wirken.

197 The cold appearance of rooms painted with a tarnished-silver type of finish can be offset by natural wood furniture with curved lines, which provides the right touch of contemporary estheticism.
Les meubles en bois naturel et aux formes ondulées compensent les ambiances froides des pièces recouvertes de peinture argentée, similaire à la couleur que prend l'argent au fil du temps. De même, ils créent une esthétique définitivement contemporaine.
In kalten Wohnumgebungen, die einen altsilbernen Anstrich haben, wirken Möbel aus Naturholz mit gewellten Linien ausgleichend. Diese Kombination schafft eine sehr zeitgemäße Ästhetik.

198 Minimalist tables of laminate and steel and folding chairs also made of steel or of black plastic are ideal for enlarging small dining rooms.
Pour agrandir visuellement les salles à manger de petites dimensions, les tables aux lignes minimalistes, faites de plaques laminées d'acier, et les sièges design, en acier ou plastique de couleur noire sont idéals.
Um kleine Speisezimmer größer wirken zu lassen, eignen sich Tische mit minimalistischen Linien aus gewalzten Stahlplatten und Designerstühle, die ebenfalls aus Stahl oder aus schwarzem Kunststoff sein können.

199 Vinyl decals with silvery motifs on gray or black backgrounds give life to transitional spaces such as halls and corridors.
Les adhésifs en vinyle aux motifs de couleur argent, sur fond gris ou noir, accentuent la mise en valeur des espaces de circulation, entrées ou couloirs.

198

Vinylaufkleber mit silbernen Motiven auf grauem oder schwarzem Hintergrund unterstreichen die Rolle von Durchgangsräumen wie Eingangsbereiche oder Flure.

200 In single-space environments such as studio apartments, the kitchen area can be delineated with a strip of brushed steel.
Dans les espaces à ambiance unique, on peut délimiter la zone de la cuisine en la revêtant d'acier au fini mat.
In Wohnumgebungen mit nur einem einzigen Raum kann der Küchenbereich durch eine Stahlverkleidung mit matter Oberfläche abgegrenzt werden.

201 Chrome metal and brushed steel decorative elements play an important role in the latest interior design trends.
Les dernières tendances font appel à toutes sortes d'éléments décoratifs en argent chromé et acier poli.
Alle Arten von Dekorationselementen aus Chrom oder Edelstahl sind der neuste Trend in der Raumgestaltung.

202 Stainless steel work surfaces with a matt finish and shiny metal electrical appliances play each other off nicely in open kitchens, which acquire more generous visual proportions in the process.
Pour que les cuisines américaines paraissent plus grandes, il suffit de les revêtir d'acier inoxydable au fini mat, en contraste avec les électroménagers au fini brillant.
Um offene Küchen weiter wirken zu lassen, kann man sie mit mattem Edelstahl verkleiden und mit glänzenden Haushaltsgeräten einen Kontrast schaffen.

203 Chrome metal desk lamps are a vital component of a retro style.
Les lampes signées, chromées et argent permettent de forger un s
rétro.
Verchromte oder silberfarbene Designerlampen sind ein typisches ment des Retrostils.

204 Metallic shelves mounted on a white wall offer a discreet, unobtru presence.
Installées sur un mur blanc, les étagères métallisées paraissent légè
Metallische Regale an einer weißen Wand wirken visuell sehr leicht.

Multicolor
Multicolore
Bunt

214

205 A variety of colors inject cheerfulness into a living space.
La variété des couleurs contribue à créer des ambiances joyeuses et pleines de vie.
Durch die Kombination verschiedener Farben entstehen fröhliche und lebendige Räume.

206 The important thing to take into account when combining tones is that they must belong to the same chromatic range to avoid reducing space.
L'unique condition à respecter, est de s'assurer que les combinaisons de tons restent dans la même gamme chromatique. Sinon, les univers tendront à se réduire visuellement.
Die einzige Regel, die man dabei berücksichtigen muss, ist, dass alle miteinander kombinierten Töne zur gleichen Farbskala gehören müssen. Andernfalls wirken die Räume visuell kleiner.

207 Multicolored runner rugs with a horizontal stripe pattern make narrow corridors and passageways look a lot wider.
Les tapis multicolores aux rayures horizontales élargissent les couloirs étroits.
Bunte Teppiche mit horizontalen Streifen lassen enge Flure weiter wirken.

208 On the other hand, large, ethnic-style rugs with intricate and colorful motifs tend to make environments heavier and should therefore be avoided.
D'un autre côté, les grands tapis de style ethnique, au graphique complexe et couleurs variées, chargeant trop l'ambiance, sont à éviter.

Andererseits lassen große Teppiche im ethnischen Stil mit comple grafischen Mustern und verschiedenen Farben die Umgebung sch überladen wirken; deshalb sollte man sie besser vermeiden.

209 Wallpapers in different pastel shades lighten up a room when comb with a white ceiling and a pale stained parquet flooring.
Conjugués avec un plafond blanc et un parquet de bois clair, les pap muraux, dans différents tons pastel, apportent de la luminosité.
Tapeten in verschiedenen Pastelltönen lassen den Raum heller wir wenn man sie mit einer weißen Decke und Parkettboden aus hellem I kombiniert.

210 Upholstery with large floral patterns makes items of furniture look sma
Les revêtements aux grands motifs floraux réduisent visuellemer taille des meubles.
Bezüge mit großen Blumenmotiven lassen die Möbel optisch kleiner wir

211 Chairs of the same model but of different colors around a natural w dining table tend to give the dining room a more personal touch.
Afin d'apporter une touche personnelle à la salle à manger, on peut c sir des sièges du même modèle, mais en bois naturel.
Um ein Speisezimmer persönlicher zu gestalten, kann man Stühle gleichen Modells in verschiedenen Farben wählen und diese um ei Esstisch aus Holz aufstellen.

212 A set of brightly colored towels neatly folded and stacked on a s can give traditional bathrooms with white tiling and fixtures a cont porary feel.

205

Les anciennes salles de bains, aux dalles et sanitaires blancs, prendront des allures contemporaines, en disposant, bien en vue sur une étagère, des serviettes de couleurs intenses, pliées l'une sur l'autre.
Alte Bäder mit weißen Kacheln und Toiletten wirken moderner, wenn man auf einem Regal in Augenhöhe Handtücher in starken Farben stapelt.

3 A display of glass vases in various colors on a console table is sure to become the focus of attention in any environment.
Une console ornée d'une série de vases en verre de différentes couleurs, sera le point de mire de n'importe quel espace.
Eine Konsole, die mit Glaskrügen in verschiedenen Farben dekoriert ist, zieht in jeder Umgebung die Blicke auf sich.

4 A wall with a multicolored checkered pattern makes for a cheerful children's room.
Un mur divisé en carrés de couleurs diverses, crée une chambre à coucher d'enfants très gaie.
Durch eine Wand, die in verschiedene bunte Rechtecke unterteilt ist, entsteht ein heiteres Kinderzimmer.

5 A set of white shelves will become the centerpiece in a white painted room if its background is painted different colors and combined with light.
On peut peindre le fond d'une étagère (blanche, comme le reste de la chambre) en différentes couleurs qui, unies à la lumière, feront de ce meuble le point de mire de la pièce.

Man kann die Rückwand eines Regals (weiß, wie der Rest des Raumes) in verschiedenen Farben streichen, so dass dieses Möbel in Kombination mit der Beleuchtung zum Hauptdarsteller des Raumes wird.

216 Small Chinese lanterns in various colors give a touch of chic to patios and terraces.
Les lanternes chinoises de diverses couleurs donnent un air chic au patio ou à la terrasse.
Chinesische Laternen in verschiedenen Farben lassen den Innenhof oder die Terrasse schick wirken.

210

Transparencies
Transparences
Transparenz

226

217 Transparent or translucent materials are vital for providing a feeling of space in very small surroundings as they let the light through to prevent the creation of dark corners.

Les transparences sont vitales lorsqu'il s'agit de créer un sentiment d'espace dans les habitations à faibles mètres carrés : en effet, en laissant passer la lumière, elles évitent la formation de coins sombres.

Die Transparenzen sind sehr wichtig, um einem Raum das Gefühl von Weite zu geben, vor allem in kleinen Wohnungen. Sie lassen das Licht durch, so dass dunkle Winkel vermieden werden.

218 A glass sliding panel situated between a kitchen and a combined living/dining room marks out two independent environments without reducing the actual space.

Un panneau de verre coulissant, situé entre le salon-salle à manger et la cuisine, crée deux univers indépendants, sans pour autant réduire l'espace.

Eine Schiebewand aus Glas zwischen dem kombinierten Wohn- und Speisezimmer und der Küche schafft zwei unabhängige Wohnumgebungen, ohne den Raum zu verkleinern.

219 Glass or acrylic partitions and transparent plastic curtains help bathrooms with very small windows make the most of natural light.

Les paravents en verre ou acrylique et les rideaux de plastique transparent illuminent les salles de bains aux très petites fenêtres.

Trennwände aus Glas oder Acryl und transparente Plastikgardinen sorgen für Helligkeit in Bädern mit sehr kleinen Fenstern.

220 Transparent acrylic consoles are ideal for small corners.

Les consoles de méthacrylate transparent sont idéales pour les pet recoins.

Konsolen aus transparentem Metakrylat eignen sich ideal für kleine Ecke

221 In a living room that does not allow for a lot of furniture, a transpare coffee table with a built-in light gives a contemporary touch.

Dans les salons dont la taille ne permet pas d'avoir beaucoup de me bles, les tables de milieu transparentes, dotées d'un éclairage intérie apportent une touche design.

Für Wohnzimmer, in denen aufgrund ihrer geringen Größe nur wen Möbel Platz finden, eignen sich ausgezeichnet transparente Couc sche, die von innen beleuchtet sind und die so dem Raum viel Moder tät geben.

222 Acrylic ceiling lights with tear-drop glass bulbs give glamor and lightne to a sitting room.

Les plafonniers en méthacrylate, dotés de larmes de verre, confère *glamour* et légèreté aux salons.

Deckenlampen aus Metakrylat mit Glasperlen lassen das Wohnzimm glamourös und leicht wirken.

223 Inflatable transparent plastic armchairs are a good choice for small s ting rooms as they are not only discreet but can also be deflated and away when more space is required.

227

Les fauteuils gonflables, en plastique transparent, sont une option judicieuse pour les petits salons. En effet, sur le plan visuel, ils semblent très légers. De plus, ils sont facilement démontables, si l'on a besoin de plus d'espace.

Aufblasbare, transparente Kunststoffsessel sind eine gute Option für kleine Wohnzimmer, da sie visuell sehr leicht wirken und außerdem einfach entfernt werden können, wenn mehr Platz benötigt wird.

224 Glass extractor hoods take up very little space in kitchens.

Les hottes d'extraction en verre occupent très peu d'espace dans la cuisine.

Abzugshauben aus Glas nehmen in der Küche wenig Platz weg.

225 Silk-threaded or pearl-sequined curtains that catch and reflect the light can be used for windows or to divide up different areas.

Les rideaux réalisés avec des fils de soie ou des paillettes perlées, qui captent et reflètent la lumière, peuvent être installés devant les fenêtres ou utilisés pour définir les différents espaces de vie.

Man kann für Fenster und Raumteiler Gardinen aus Seidenfäden oder mit Paillettenperlen benutzen, die das Licht einfangen und reflektieren.

226 A glass washbasin mounted directly on the wall rather than on supporting furniture is ideal for a small bathroom.

Les lavabos en verre, appliqués directement sur le mur et sans meuble d'appui, sont idéals pour les petites salles de bains.

Runde Waschbecken aus Kristall, die direkt an der Wand angebracht sind und kein Untermöbel haben, eignen sich ausgezeichnet für kleine Bäder.

227 Curtains made from fine, translucent fabric let the light through without attenuating it.

Les rideaux en voile fin et transparent tamisent la lumière grâce à leur texture, sans pour autant en ôter la clarté.

Gardinen aus feinen, transparenten Stoffen dämpfen mit ihrer Textur das Licht, machen den Raum jedoch nicht dunkler.

228 In bedrooms and kitchens it is best to avoid wardrobes and cupboards with transparent doors as they do not contribute to the feeling of orderliness that is vital in reduced spaces.

Dans les chambres à coucher et dans la cuisine, il est préférable d'éviter les armoires aux portes transparentes, car elles ne permettent pas de donner l'aspect rangé nécessaire aux petits espaces.

In Schlafzimmern und Küchen sollte man Schränke mit transparenten Türen vermeiden. Sie lassen den Eindruck von Unordnung in kleinen Räumen entstehen.

222

Harmony   Harmonie   Harmonie
Contrast Contraste Kontrast Color
Gradation Tons de couleur Farbtöne
Harmony   Harmonie   Contras
Contraste Kontrast Color Gradation
Tons de couleur Farbtöne Harmony
Harmonie Contrast Contraste Color
Gradation Tons de couleur Farbtöne
Harmony   Harmonie   Harmonie
Contrast Contraste Color Gradatio
Tonsde couleur Farbtöne Harmony
Harmonie   Harmonie   Contras
Contraste Kontrast Color Gradatio
Tons de couleur Farbtöne Harmony
Harmonie   Contrast   Contraste

Color Schemes
Schémas de couleurs
Farbschemata

Colors are set out on the color wheel within the visible light spectrum. The order of the spectral colors is red, orange, yellow, green, turquoise, blue, violet and magenta. Pairs that lie at opposite sides of the wheel are contrasting or complementary colors: blue–orange, red–green, yellow–violet. In simpler, non-scientific terms, colors can be classified as 'warm'/'hot' or 'cool'/'cold', based on the sensations they arouse in human beings. Endless combinations can be created from these classifications, affecting different environments in a variety of ways.

Les couleurs se répartissent en un cercle chromatique au cœur du spectre de la lumière visible. Ce cercle se décline dans l'ordre consécutif suivant : rouge, orange, jaune, vert, turquoise, bleu, violet et magenta. Les paires diamétralement opposées à la circonférence, sont les opposées ou complémentaires : bleu-orange, rouge-vert, jaune-violet. Mais ont peut également classifier les couleurs en « chaudes » ou « froides » sans plus de connaissance que la pure sensation qu'elles produisent sur l'être humain. A partir de ces classifications, on trouve une infinité d'associations dont les conséquences se répercutent inéluctablement sur l'ambiance des espaces de vie.

Die Farben verteilen sich in einem Farbkreis innerhalb des sichtbaren Lichtspektrums. Die fortlaufende Reihenfolge ist Rot, Orange, Gelb, Grün, Türkis, Blau, Violett und Magenta. Die Paare, die sich im Farbkreis gegenüberstehen, sind die Komplementärfarben: Blau/Orange, Rot/Grün, Gelb/Violett. Aber man kann Farben auch in „warme" und „kalte" Farben unterteilen. Diese Unterteilung ist jedoch nicht wissenschaftlich belegt, sondern einfach nur auf den Eindruck zurückzuführen, den sie im Menschen erwecken. Auf Grundlage dieser Einteilungen sind eine Vielzahl von Kombinationen möglich, die unbestreitbar den Raum beeinflussen.

229

260

Harmony
Harmonie
Harmonie

238

232

229 Harmonious colors are those that work well together. They produce attractive, balanced and serene color scheme.

Les couleurs harmonieuses sont celles qui fonctionnent bien entre elle Elles produisent un schéma de couleur attrayant, équilibré et apaisa pour le regard.

Harmonische Farben sind solche, die gut zueinander passen. Durch s entsteht ein anziehendes, ausgeglichenes und auf das Auge beruhige wirkendes Farbkonzept.

230 The chromatic color wheel is an invaluable tool for determining harm ny. Colors are distributed according to the segment of light visible in t solar spectrum. Both black and white are excluded.

Le cercle chromatique est un outil précieux pour créer l'harmonie. L couleurs sont distribuées selon le segment de lumière visible du spect solaire. Le blanc et le noir en sont exclus.

Der Farbkreis ist ein wertvolles Instrument, um Farben harmonisch a einander abzustimmen. Die Farben sind in Abhängigkeit von ihrem Ant des sichtbaren Lichtes im Sonnenspektrum verteilt. Weiß und Schwa sind ausgeschlossen.

231 According to this system, the primary colors are yellow, blue and re The secondary colors are those resulting from mixing two of the prima colors together (orange, green and violet).

Selon ce schéma, les couleurs primaires sont le jaune, le bleu et rouge. Les secondaires sont celles qui naissent du mélange de de couleurs primaires (orange, vert et violet).

233

Nach diesem Konzept sind die Primärfarben Gelb, Blau und Rot. Die Sekundärfarben sind die, die aus der Mischung der Primärfarben entstehen (Orange, Grün und Violett).

232 Warm or hot colors, i.e. yellow, orange and red, create welcoming surroundings.
Les couleurs chaudes, c'est-à-dire, le jaune, l'orange et le rouge, créent des ambiances accueillantes.
Die warmen Farben, also Gelb, Orange und Rot, schaffen eine freundliche Atmosphäre.

233 Cool or cold colors, on the other hand, impart serenity to living spaces and coolness to areas that get a lot of sunlight. These colors are violet, blue, turquoise and green.
Par contre, les couleurs froides dotent les pièces de sérénité et rafraîchissent les zones très ensoleillées. Ce sont le violet, le bleu, le turquoise et le vert.
Im Gegensatz dazu machen kalte Farben den Raum gelassener und wirken erfrischend in Bereichen, in die viel Sonnenlicht einfällt. Die kalten Farben sind Violett, Blau, Türkis und Grün.

234 Using any color as a starting point, one can draw an equilateral triangle on the color wheel. Thus the primaries form a harmonious trio in the same way as the secondary colors, but combinations of these two groups are not often used as they do not go well together.

Prenant comme point de départ n'importe quelle couleur, on peut tracer un triangle isocèle dans le cercle chromatique. Ainsi, les couleurs primaires forment un trio harmonieux, identique aux secondaires. Ces combinaisons s'utilisent relativement peu, car elles se heurtent entre elles.
Wenn man als Ausgangspunkt irgendeine Farbe nimmt, kann man ein gleichseitiges Dreieck im Farbkreis zeichnen. So formen die Primärfarben ein harmonisches Trio, ebenso wie die Sekundärfarben. Diese Kombination von beiden Gruppen wird relativ selten benutzt, denn sie beißen sich.

235 If various colors are to be used in different parts of the house, it is a good idea to use those that are next to each other on the wheel, e.g. indigo blue for the bedroom, acid green for the kitchen and bathroom and lilac for the sitting room.
Si l'on veut employer des couleurs distinctes dans les diverses parties de la maison, préférer plutôt celles qui sont voisines dans le spectre. Par exemple : le bleu indigo est idéal pour les chambres à coucher, le vert acidulé pour la cuisine ou la salle de bains, et le lilas pour le salon.
Wenn Sie verschiedene Farben in verschiedenen Teilen des Hauses benutzen möchten, sollten Sie Farben verwenden, die im Spektrum nebeneinander liegen, zum Beispiel Indigoblau eignet sich gut für die Schlafzimmer, Gelbgrün für die Küche und das Bad, und Lila für das Wohnzimmer.

236 The same principle can be applied to furniture. In this case, however, the object is to create the illusion of space by using colors properly.
On peut appliquer le même principe au mobilier d'une chambre. Dans ce cas, en fonction de la bonne utilisation des couleurs, on peut tenter d'accroître la sensation d'espace.

229

Das gleiche Prinzip kann man auf die Möbel eines Raumes anwenden. In diesem Fall wird versucht, durch die richtige Anwendung der Farben den Eindruck von mehr Raum entstehen zu lassen.

237 When applying chromatic combinations in the same room, the strongest color should be kept for the most important pieces of furniture.

Lorsque l'on réalise des combinaisons chromatiques dans une même pièce, il faut que la couleur dominante soit réservée aux pièces importantes du mobilier.

Wenn man Farben innerhalb des gleichen Raumes kombiniert, sollte man die stärkeren Farben für die wichtigen Möbelstücke verwenden.

238 The base color is the one that is used most extensively and sets off the others. The accent color complements the base color and gives a dash of audacity to the color scheme. The complementary color is usually found next to the accent color on the color wheel.

La couleur dominante, plus étendue, sert à faire ressortir les autres couleurs. La tonique, est complémentaire de la couleur dominante et apporte la touche audacieuse. La couleur de médiation est généralement voisine de la tonique dans le cercle chromatique.

Die dominante Farbe ist jene, die die größte Fläche einnimmt, und sie dient dazu, die anderen Farben hervorzuheben. Die akzentuierende Farbe ist jene, die die dominante Farbe ergänzt und ihr die geeignete Note gibt. Die vermittelnde Farbe liegt üblicherweise neben der akzentuierenden Farbe im Farbkreis.

239 In a harmonious composition in which pale green is the base color (walls), and pink the accent one (rugs), the complementing color can be lilac (sofa).

Dans une composition harmonieuse où la couleur dominante est le v clair (murs) et le rose la tonique (tapis), le médiateur peut alors être lilas (divan).

In einer harmonischen Komposition, in der die dominierende Farbe H grün ist (Wände) und Rosa die akzentuierende Farbe (Teppiche), ka die vermittelnde Farbe Lila sein (Diwan).

240 Ochers, oranges and pinks work best for small, much used spaces, the furniture must be in harmony with these colors.

Dans les petits espaces très empruntés, les tons d'ocre, orange et r sont idéals, s'ils sont en harmonie avec les meubles.

Für kleine Räume, die viel benutzt werden, eignen sich Ocker-, Oran und Rosatöne, zu denen die Möbel farblich passen müssen.

241 Blues, greens and violets are acceptable for large spaces.

Les plus grands espaces acceptent les bleus, verts et violets.

In größeren Räumen kann man Blau-, Grün- und Violetttöne verwend

242 The best combining colors for wood-dominated environments are the close to orange, i.e. green, yellow, red and pink.

Dans les espaces où le bois domine, les couleurs voisines se mari mieux avec l'orange, à savoir : les teintes de vert, jaune, rouge et ros

Zu Räumen, in denen Holz dominiert, passen besser Farben, die ne Orange liegen wie Grün, Gelb, Rot und Rosa.

Contrast
Contraste
Kontrast

254

255

243 Contrast occurs in compositions where the colors are completely ⊙ similar.

Il y a contraste lorsque dans une composition les couleurs n'ont aucu similarité.

Ein Kontrast entsteht, wenn Farben miteinander kombiniert werden, keinerlei Ähnlichkeit haben, z. B. Orange und Blau.

244 Combining colors that are in opposition on the color wheel brir dynamism to a space, but can prove overpowering if they are both gi the same strength.

Combiner des couleurs opposées dans le cercle chromatique imprèg les pièces de dynamisme, mais peut être étouffant si les deux on même importance.

Wenn man die Farben miteinander kombiniert, die sich im Farbkr gegenüberliegen, schafft man dynamische Räume, die aber bedrücke wirken können, wenn beide Farben zu gleichen Teilen benutzt werder

245 The inclusion of neutrals, such as white paint or beige, softens lighter contrast between the primary and the secondary colors on chromatic wheel.

L'intégration de couleurs neutres, comme le blanc ou le beige, allèg le poids du contraste des couleurs primaires avec les secondaires op sées dans le cercle chromatique.

Wenn man neutrale Farben wie Weiß oder helles Holz einbezieht, w der Kontrast zwischen Primärfarben und Sekundärfarben, die im Fa kreis gegenüberliegen, etwas schwächer.

A strong combination of red and green, for example, can be softened by wood or toned down by turning the red into a pink with a dash of white.
Par exemple, la combinaison de rouge et vert s'équilibre avec le bois ou prend une teinte moins stricte si le blanc fait dériver le rouge vers le rose.
So kann man zum Beispiel die Kombination von Rot mit Grün durch Holz ausgleichen oder sie weniger streng machen, wenn Weiß das Rot in Rosa übergehen lässt.

The best example of chiaroscuro is the pairing of black and white. As neither color is part of the color wheel, their combination is always a success.
Le contraste de clair-obscur trouve son paroxysme dans le binôme blanc et noir. Comme il s'agit de couleurs hors du cercle chromatique, leur mariage est toujours réussi.
In dem Kontrast Hell-Dunkel findet das Binom Weiß und Schwarz seinen stärksten Ausdruck. Da es sich um Farben handelt, die außerhalb des Farbkreises angesiedelt sind, ist diese Kombination immer erfolgreich.

A composition made up of various shades of a single color creates warm, welcoming spaces. One basic color is used but with different levels of intensity and saturation.
Les contrastes de ton utilisent diverses nuances chromatiques et créent des pièces accueillantes. Il s'agit d'une même couleur de base, mais à un niveau différent de luminosité et saturation.
Farbkontraste, die durch verschiedene Farbnuancen entstehen, schaffen einladende, warme Räume. Es handelt sich um die gleiche Grundfarbe, aber in unterschiedlicher Helligkeit und Sättigung.

249 These combinations can make a room appear longer or shorter.
Ces agencements permettent d'élargir ou de rapetisser visuellement un espace.
Diese Kombinationen machen den Raum visuell länger oder kürzer.

250 Using a warm, deep color for the wall at the far end of a long room and a light one for the others will make the room look squarer: red and pink, for example.
Pour qu'une pièce tout en longueur paraisse plus carrée, peindre le mur du fond d'une couleur chaude foncée et réserver les tons clairs pour le reste. Exemple : rouge et rose.
Damit ein länglicher Raum quadratischer wirkt, sollte man die hintere Wand in einer warmen, dunklen Farbe streichen und die übrigen Wände in hellen Farben, z. B. Rot und Rosa.

251 To obtain the opposite result, three of the walls should be painted a deeper color and the fourth a light one: blue and turquoise, for example.
Pour obtenir l'effet contraire, peindre trois murs dans une teinte foncée et la quatrième d'une teinte plus claire. Exemple : bleu et turquoise.
Um die gegenteilige Wirkung zu erreichen, muss man die drei anderen Wände in einem dunklen Ton und die hintere Wand heller streichen, z. B. in Blau und Türkis.

252 It is best to reserve strongly contrasting color schemes for dynamic spaces such as kitchens and dining rooms. More harmonious combinations have a positive effect on mood, and therefore are more suited for bedrooms and living rooms.

252

Il est conseillé de réserver les contrastes pour les espaces dynamiques, comme la cuisine ou la salle à manger. Les harmonies chromatiques ont plus d'effets sur les états d'âme : elles sont donc idéales pour les chambres à coucher et salons.

Es ist empfehlenswert, Kontraste in den dynamischeren Räumen wie Küche und Esszimmer zu verwenden. Die harmonischen Farben haben eine wohltuende Wirkung auf den Gemütszustand, deshalb eignen sie sich gut für Schlaf- und Wohnzimmer.

253   In an open studio or loft color contrasts can be used to delineate the different zones.

Dans un studio ou un loft, on peut recourir au contraste de couleurs pour définir les univers.

In einer Studiowohnung oder einem Loft kann man Farbkontraste benutzen, um die verschiedenen Wohnumgebungen zu definieren.

254   The optical effect produced by black-and-white wallpapers makes the walls look larger.

Les papiers peints aux motifs blancs et noirs, créent un effet d'optique qui agrandit visuellement les murs.

Tapeten mit schwarz-weißen Motiven haben eine optische Wirkung, die die Wände visuell vergrößert.

255   Rugs with a different color from that of the floor help mark out various areas.

Les tapis dont la couleur contraste avec celle du sol, permettent de délimiter les diverses sphères de vie.

Teppiche, deren Farbe mit dem Boden kontrastiert, dienen zur Begzung von verschiedenen Bereichen.

256   Gray is a good background color to complement strong color combtions in furniture.

Le gris est une bonne couleur de fond pour supporter la dialectiqu couleurs des meubles.

Die Farbe Grau ist ein guter Grundton, um die Wechselwirkung zwis den Farben der Möbel zu unterdrücken.

243

Color Gradation
Tons de couleur
Farbtöne

260

257 When you mix each color on the wheel with white, to make it paler, or with black, to make it deeper, its tone, value and shade are altered.

En mélangeant chacune des couleurs du cercle chromatique avec du blanc, pour plus de luminosité, ou avec du noir, pour la foncer, on en modifie le ton, la valeur ou la nuance.

Wenn man eine Farbe des Farbkreises mit Weiß mischt, um sie heller zu machen, oder mit Schwarz, damit sie dunkler wird, verändert man den Ton, den Wert oder die Nuance.

258 One tonal combination consists in using only one color and its different shades, for instance burgundy, red and pink, or dark green, acid green and pale green.

Une des possibles combinaisons tonales est d'utiliser une couleur unique et ses nuances : par exemple bordeaux, rouge et rose; vert anglais, vert acidulé, vert clair.

Eine der möglichen Kombinationen von Tönen besteht darin, eine einzige Farbe und ihre Nuancen zu benutzen, zum Beispiel Bordeauxrot, Rot und Rosa, Englischgrün, Gelbgrün und Hellgrün.

259 Combinations of different colors in their pale shades work well together. The same is true as well with combinations of deep shades.

On peut également combiner les couleurs en utilisant uniquement des nuances claires, ou sombres, de plusieurs couleurs.

Man kann auch nur helle oder nur dunkle Töne verschiedener Farben miteinander kombinieren.

260 Compositions that involve pale shades are suitable for small rooms and dark spaces as they help carry natural light.

Les compositions de tons suaves sont idéales dans les petites cham ou pour apporter la lumière du jour aux espaces sombres.

Die Kompositionen mit sanften Tönen eignen sich gut für kleine Räu oder um Licht in dunkle Räume zu bringen.

261 Deeper tints should only be used for large spaces with big openings Les tons foncés sont uniquement valables dans les grands espaces larges ouvertures.

Dunkle Töne sollte man nur in weiten Räumen mit großen Fens benutzen.

262 Glass vases and lamps are a good way to brighten up environme dominated by deeper tones.

Les vases et les lampes de verre sont une bonne solution pour illum les espaces de vie dominés par les tons foncés.

Krüge und Lampen aus Kristall sind eine gute Lösung, um Glan Wohnumgebungen zu bringen, die von dunklen Tönen beherrscht si

263 Pale warm colors are synonymous with the serene and feminine maintain their character only two of them should be used at once example: pink and ocher.

Les tons clairs chauds engendrent des univers sereins et féminins. leur donner du caractère, n'utiliser que deux couleurs, par exemple et ocre.

Warme, helle Töne schaffen eine gelassene und feminine Atmosph Um einem Raum mehr Persönlichkeit zu geben, sollte man jedoch zwei Farben benutzen, z. B. Rosa und Ocker.

Cool colors (blue, pale green and lilac) produce a sensation of distance that is ideal for very small rooms. Their use should be restricted to bedrooms and bathrooms.

Les couleurs froides (bleu, vert clair et lilas) produisent un effet de profondeur approprié aux pièces à faible superficie. Les réserver aux chambres à coucher et salles de bains.

Kalte Farben (Blau, Hellgrün und Lila) haben eine vergrößernde Wirkung, deshalb eignen sie sich gut für kleine Räume. Man sollte diese Farben für Schlaf- und Badezimmer verwenden.

Deep warm colors are recommended for gloomy rooms as they generate light and warmth. Their dynamism makes them suitable for kitchens and children's bedrooms.

Les couleurs chaudes foncées sont indiquées pour les chambres sombres, pour leur apport de lumière et de chaleur. De par leur dynamisme, les appliquer de préférence dans les cuisines et chambres d'enfants.

Warme, dunkle Farben eignen sich gut für dunkle Räume, denn sie bringen Licht und Wärme in den Raum. Da sie sehr dynamisch wirken, passen sie gut in Küchen und Kinderzimmer.

Dark, cool colors have great decorating potential but are best applied to furniture or combined with paler colors to lighten up environments.

Les couleurs froides foncées ont un grand pouvoir de décoration, mais il est préférable de ne les appliquer que sur les meubles, ou de les associer à des couleurs claires pour alléger l'espace.

Kalte, dunkle Farben sind sehr dekorativ, aber man sollte sie nur für Möbel benutzen oder sie mit hellen Farben kombinieren, damit der Raum nicht bedrückend wirkt.

267 The combination of various pastel shades is relaxing and imparts tranquillity. For this reason it is often used in the decoration of nursery rooms.

Le mariage de plusieurs tons pastel relaxe et inspire le calme. C'est pourquoi, on les utilise pour décorer les chambres à coucher de bébés.

Die Kombination von verschiedenen Pastelltönen wirkt entspannend und beruhigend, deshalb eignet sie sich für Babyzimmer.

268 The different tones of a single color can be combined with printed fabrics. Red curtains, for example, go well with a pink striped wallpaper.

Différents tons d'une même couleur admettent l'association d'imprimés. Ainsi, par exemple, les rideaux rouges vont bien avec un revêtement de mur à rayures roses.

Die verschiedenen Nuancen einer Farbe lassen die Kombination mit bedruckten Materialien zu. So kann man die roten Gardinen gut mit einer rosagestreiften Tapete kombinieren.

Single Color Effect Effets d'une couleur unique **Wirkung eine** einzigen Farbe Color and Materials Couleur et matière **Farbe und Material** Color and Light **Couleur e** lumière **Farbe und Licht** Quality and Quantity Qualité et quantité **Qualitä und Quantität** Color and Ambience Couleur et ambiance **Farbe und Ambiente** Continuity Continuite **Kontinuität** Styles Styles **Stile** Single Color Effect Effets d'une couleu unique **Wirkung einer einzigen Farbe** Color and Materials Couleur e matière **Farbe und Material** Colo

Color Effects
Effets de couleur
Die Wirkung von Farben

Color is one of the most effective tools in architecture and interior design. The combinations of colors and their interaction with materials are not only able to enlarge or reduce space, alter the height of ceilings, set off walls and make corridors appear longer, they can also transmit light to the darkest corners and modify the size – even the shape – of volumes. The power of color over environments and objects is so great that mastering its language is one of the easiest and cheapest ways of transforming an apartment or a house.

La couleur est un des outils les plus efficaces de l'architecture et du design d'intérieur. Ses associations et son interaction sur les matériaux peuvent agrandir ou réduire les univers de vie, rehausser ou abaisser les plafonds, séparer les murs ou modifier la longueur des couloirs. Mais aussi apporter de la lumière aux coins les plus sombres ou modifier la taille — et même la forme — des volumes. Son impact sur les espaces de vie et sur les objets est si important, que maîtriser le langage des couleurs constitue une des formes les plus économiques et faciles de transformer une habitation.

Farbe ist eines der effizientesten Gestaltungsmittel in der Innenarchitektur und Architektur. Die Kombination und Interaktion der Farbe mit den Materialien ermöglicht es, Räume kleiner oder größer und Decken höher oder tiefer wirken zu lassen. Ebenso kann man mit Farben Wände trennen oder einen Flur optisch verlängern oder verkürzen. Mit Farben kann man Licht in dunkle Winkel bringen oder die Größe und sogar die Form von Körpern scheinbar verändern. Der Einfluss der Farben auf die Umgebung und Objekte ist so groß, dass die gute Kenntnis der Farbeigenschafen eine preisgünstige und einfach umzusetzende Möglichkeit ist, Räume zu gestalten.

275

292

Single Color Effect
Effets d'une couleur unique
Wirkung einer einzigen Farbe

271

269 Monochromatic compositions are liable to create rather dull, character-less surroundings.

Les compositions monochromatiques courent le risque de créer des ambiances monotones, dépourvues de personnalité.

Durch einfarbige Kompositionen kann ein langweiliger und unpersönli-cher Raum entstehen.

270 The use of different textures alleviates the monotony and provides con-trast.

Pour atténuer les effets de monotonie, on peut recourir à divers types de textures, créant ainsi un contraste.

Um dieser Monotonie entgegenzuwirken, kann man verschiedene Textu-ren benutzen, durch die ein Kontrast entsteht.

271 Another possibility is to resort to tones that lie opposite to one another in the same color range, e.g. a very pale blue and a very dark blue. This will make the space with the deeper tint stand out from the rest.

On peut aussi avoir recours à des nuances de couleur très distantes, par exemple bleu très clair et bleu très foncé. Cela permet de faire ressortir la partie de la pièce peinte dans une teinte plus sombre.

Eine andere Möglichkeit ist es, sehr weit auseinander liegende Farbnu-ancen zu benutzen, z. B. ein sehr helles und ein sehr dunkles Blau. So kann man den Teil des Raumes, der dunkler gestrichen ist, hervorheben.

272 Using the deepest tone of a color for the furniture and the palest for the walls will give the former more prominence and create a somewhat lighter neobaroque style.

Pour faire ressortir les meubles, les peindre dans un ton plus foncé les murs d'un ton plus clair. C'est la bonne solution pour créer un s néo-baroque peu chargé.

Um Möbel hervorzuheben, kann man sie in einem dunkleren Ton und Wände heller streichen. Diese Lösung eignet sich ausgezeichnet, einen neobarocken, aber nicht überladenen Stil zu schaffen.

273 Moldings painted a lighter tone than walls bring a space look brigh The same principle can be applied to curtains.

En peignant les moulures d'un ton plus clair que les murs, on obtier une plus grande luminosité dans la pièce. On peut appliquer le mê principe aux rideaux.

Wenn man ein Gesims in einem helleren Ton benutzt, wirkt der Ra auch heller. Das gleiche Prinzip kann man bei Gardinen anwenden.

274 One of the advantages of a monochromatic scheme is that it give feeling of continuity. It is a very good way of integrating different ar into the same living space.

Un des avantages du schéma monochromatique, c'est l'obtention d espace fluide. C'est donc une solution optimale pour intégrer diver ambiances au sein d'une même habitation.

Ein Vorteil des einfarbigen Konzeptes ist, dass es den Raum durch hend wirken lässt. Deshalb ist es eine gute Lösung, um verschied Umgebungen in einer einzigen Wohnung zu integrieren.

275 Warm tones are best for zones of activity such as dining rooms or dren's rooms, while pale, cool colors are more suitable for areas signed for rest as they encourage relaxation.

279

Dans les zones actives comme les salles à manger ou les chambres d'enfant, les couleurs chaudes sont de mise. Pour les zones de repos les couleurs froides et claires sont mieux appropriées, car elles ont un pouvoir relaxant.
Die aktiven Bereiche, wie das Speisezimmer oder die Kinderzimmer, sollte man in warmen Farben gestalten. Für Ruhezonen eignen sich helle, kalte Farben besser, denn sie wirken entspannend.

76 Choosing white as an overall color imposes simplicity, brightness and elegance.
Le choix du blanc comme couleur générale dégage simplicité, luminosité et élégance.
Wenn man Weiß als Grundfarbe wählt, erzeugt dies Einfachheit, Helligkeit und Eleganz.

77 White can be used for the flooring throughout the house.
Le blanc est une couleur à utiliser sur tous les sols d'une maison.
Weiß ist eine Farbe, die man für alle Böden des Hauses benutzen kann.

78 Black is useful as a common color to set off structural elements such as beams, columns and staircases.
Le noir peut être appliqué comme couleur de base pour rehausser tous les éléments structuraux, à l'instar des poutres, colonnes et escaliers.
Schwarz kann man dazu benutzen, alle Strukturelemente wie Balken, Säulen und Treppen hervorzuheben.

79 Deep tones tend to make the walls look further away, creating depth. Pale ones have the opposite effect.

Les tons sombres tendent à éloigner visuellement les murs, créant de la profondeur, et les tons clairs les rapprochent.
Dunkle Farben entfernen die Wände visuell; sie schaffen Tiefe. Helle Farben bringen die Wände optisch näher.

280 When the floor is the darkest element in a house, it gives the illusion of space.
Si le sol affiche la couleur plus foncée, les pièces sembleront alors plus spacieuses.
Wenn der Boden einen dunkleren Ton als die Wände hat, wirken die Räume größer.

270

Color and Materials
Couleur et matière
Farbe und Material

287

281

281 When applied to a particular material, a color's effect can be altered s nificantly depending on the material's ability to absorb or reflect light
Une couleur peut changer radicalement en fonction de la compositi de la matière sur laquelle elle s'applique et des différentes capacit d'absorption ou d'émission de lumière.
Die Komposition eines Materials kann durch Farbe grundlegend verä dert werden. Ausschlaggebend dabei ist dessen Fähigkeit, das Licht a zunehmen oder widerzuspiegeln.

282 Glossy paints reflect more light than matt ones, giving the actual co greater presence.
Les peintures brillantes dégagent plus de lumière que les mates, renf çant ainsi la présence de la couleur.
Glänzende Anstriche reflektieren mehr Licht als matte Farben, desha verleihen sie der Farbe eine stärkere Wirkung.

283 Porous materials and matt paints tend to make colors look warmer.
Les matières poreuses et les peintures mates tendent à être plus chaud Poröse Materialien und matte Farben wirken meist wärmer.

284 White-painted wood floors are easy to combine with any style of furnitu
Les sols de bois peints en blanc sont plus faciles à marier avec tous styles de meubles.
Böden, die mit weiß gestrichenem Holz belegt sind, lassen sich einfa mit Möbeln jeder Stilrichtung kombinieren.

285 Polished, shiny flooring materials create a sensation of greater spa with their reflective qualities.

283

Les carrelages, aux effets miroir, agrandissent les pièces.
Spiegelnde Fußbodenbeläge aus Naturstein oder mit Zementglattstrich lassen den Raum größer wirken.

6 Gray concrete absorbs a large amount of light and should therefore only be used as flooring material for spaces of generous proportions.
Le béton gris absorbant beaucoup de lumière, ce type de revêtement est donc uniquement approprié pour les très grands espaces.
Grauer Beton absorbiert mehr Licht, deshalb sollte man diese Verkleidung nur für sehr große Räume verwenden.

7 Paints with a metallic finish have great light-reflecting properties, which make them particularly suitable for dark corridors and corners.
Les peintures avec des scintillements métalliques, reflétant davantage la lumière, peuvent être une bonne solution pour les couloirs et les coins sombres.
Farben mit metallischem Schimmer reflektieren viel Licht. Deshalb eignen sie sich gut für dunkle Flure und Ecken.

8 Colors acquire a softer tone on thick-grain leather furniture.
Les couleurs prennent un ton plus discret sur les meubles en peau opaque.
An Möbeln aus opakem Leder wirken die Farben gedeckter.

9 Colored glass lamps and wall lights stand out a lot more than those made of ceramic.
Les lampes et appliques de lumière en verre de couleur sont davantage mises en valeur que celles en céramique.

Lampen und Wandlampen aus buntem Glas haben eine stärkere Wirkung als Keramiklampen.

290 A combination of light colored textured tiles makes small bathrooms come to life.
Pour donner vie aux petites salles de bains, on peut mélanger les céramiques texturées dans une couleur claire.
Um kleine Bäder lebendiger zu gestalten, kann man texturierte Keramik in einer hellen Farbe kombinieren.

291 Both bright and pale colors are acceptable on draperies made of sheer fabrics that let a lot of light through, even on small windows.
Les toiles, aux textures légères, laissent passer la lumière, et peuvent donc être de couleurs intenses, même si les fenêtres sont petites.
Stoffe mit leichter Textur lassen das Licht durch. Deshalb kann man auch dann kräftige Farben wählen, wenn die Fenster klein sind.

292 Lacquer finished wood furniture should always be painted in dramatic color combinations.
Les meubles en bois laqué appellent des associations de couleurs intenses.
Für Möbel aus lackiertem Holz sind Kombinationen von kräftigen Farben zu empfehlen.

281

282

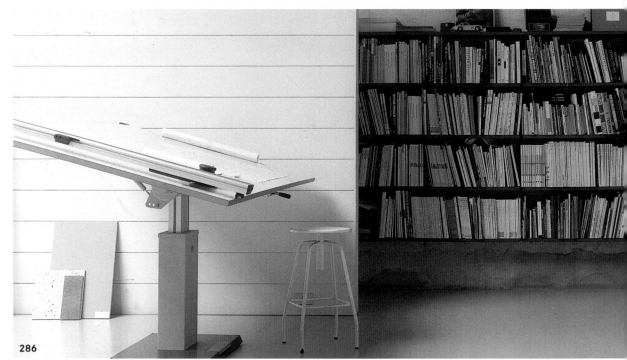

286

Color and Light
Couleur et lumière
Farbe und Licht

301

293 As colors vary with the light, it is advisable to paint test swaths in various areas before painting a room.

La lumière modifie l'apparence des couleurs. Avant de peindre une chambre, il est donc conseillé de faire des essais sur des petites surfaces.

Das Licht verändert das Aussehen der Farbe, deshalb sollte man, bevor man den ganzen Raum streicht, erst die Farbe auf kleineren Flächen ausprobieren.

294 Natural and white light acquire the color of a painted surface. An ocher-painted wall in a room, for example, will make the entire space look ocher.

Les surfaces de couleur font que la lumière naturelle ou blanche adopte cette même couleur. Par exemple, dans une chambre un seul mur peint en ocre peut teinter tout l'espace d'ocre.

Farbige Flächen bewirken, dass das Tageslicht oder weißes Licht diese Farbe annehmen. Wenn zum Beispiel in einem Raum eine einzige Wand in der Farbe Ocker gestrichen ist, nimmt die ganze Umgebung diesen Farbton an.

295 Colored lighting against a colored wall can deepen, lighten or alter the tint. For example, magenta lighting gives a yellow wall an orange tone.

Un éclairage coloré sur un mur de couleur peut intensifier, altérer ou inverser la couleur. A titre d'exemple, un mur jaune prendra un ton orange avec une lumière magenta.

Eine farbige Beleuchtung über einer bunten Wand kann die Farbe intensivieren, verändern oder umkehren. So kann zum Beispiel eine gelbe Wand einen Orangeton annehmen, wenn sie mit magentafarbenem Licht beleuchtet wird.

296 In a similar way, amber lighting will give a blue wall a green appearan

De même, un mur bleu se transformera en vert, si on lui appliqu éclairage de couleur ambre.

Auf die gleiche Weise wird eine blaue Wand zu einer grünen, wenn r bernsteinfarbenes Licht verwendet.

297 White light has three ranges: cold for lights that have a bluish tone orescent), neutral for those that give off a white light (halogen lam and warm for those with a yellowish tone (incandescent bulbs).

La lumière blanche possède trois degrés d'apparence : froide pour les qui ont un ton blanc bleuté (fluorescentes), neutre pour celles donnent une lumière blanche (spots halogènes), et chaude pour ce qui ont un ton blanc jaunâtre (ampoules à incandescence).

Weißes Licht hat drei Abstufungen in seinem Aussehen. Es wirkt k wenn es sich um bläuliches Weiß handelt (Leuchtstoffröhren), neu wenn es rein weiß ist (Halogenleuchten) und warm, wenn es gelb leuchtet (Glühbirne).

298 To give a welcoming feel to a totally white environment, it is necess to use fixtures that give off a warm white light and to avoid fluoresc lights.

Pour que les espaces d'un blanc immaculé restent accueillants, il conseillé d'utiliser la lumière blanche chaude des ampoules et d'élim les fluorescentes.

Damit völlig weiße Räume freundlicher wirken, sollte man das wa Licht von Glühbirnen wählen und Leuchtstoffröhren vermeiden.

294

9 Another option is to use red, amber or orange acrylic or glass shades.
Une autre solution est d'utiliser les lampes en méthacrylate ou en verre de couleur rouge, ambre ou orange.
Eine andere Möglichkeit ist, Lampen aus Metakrylat oder Glas in den Farben Rot, Bernstein oder Orange zu wählen.

0 Blues and greens look rather grayish and dull under the warm white light of incandescent bulbs, but they become bright and luminous when illuminated by fluorescent tubes.
Les couleurs bleues et vertes apparaissent plutôt grisâtres et ternes sous la lumière blanche et chaude des ampoules incandescentes. Sous la lumière des tubes fluorescents, les bleus et les verts apparaissent clairs et lumineux.
Blaue und grüne Töne sehen meist gräulich und glanzlos unter dem warmen Licht von Glühbirnen aus. Blau- und Grüntöne wirken klarer und leuchtender, wenn sie mit Leuchtstoffröhren beleuchtet werden.

1 The reverse phenomenon occurs with yellow and red tints, so it is advisable to use incandescent bulbs rather than fluorescents.
Avec les teintes jaunes et rouges, c'est le phénomène contraire qui se produit. Utiliser donc de préférence les ampoules à la place de l'éclairage fluorescent.
Mit gelben und roten Farben geschieht das Gegenteil, für sie sollte man ebenfalls besser Glühbirnen statt Leuchtstoffröhren verwenden.

2 The same paint can vary dramatically from one room to another. For example, the same yellow used in a space that gets a lot of natural light and in one with little light will look like two distinct colors.

Une même peinture appliquée dans deux chambres peut avoir des résultats différents. Par exemple : le même jaune appliqué dans une pièce inondée de lumière du jour et aussi dans une autre plus sombre, donnera deux couleurs différentes.
Wenn man die gleiche Farbe in zwei verschiedenen Räumen verwendet, kann man verschiedene Ergebnisse erzielen. Zum Beispiel kann das gleiche Gelb in einem Raum, in den viel Licht fällt, ganz anders aussehen, wenn es in einem dunklen Raum verwendet wird.

303 If lighting of a different color is chosen for each room of a house, it will help the various rooms stand out from one another.
L'éclairage des espaces avec des cônes de lumière de différentes couleurs sépare visuellement les zones les unes des autres.
Die Beleuchtung verschiedener Zonen mit Lichtkegeln in unterschiedlichen Farben trennt verschiedene Bereiche visuell voneinander ab.

304 Using a number of small white spotlights, rather than a single light source for an entire room, is an elegant touch for black walls.
Pour que les murs noirs gagnent en élégance, il est conseillé d'appliquer divers points de lumière très blanche au lieu d'une seule source d'éclairage pour toute la pièce.
Damit schwarze Wände elegant wirken, sollte man verschiedene Lichtpunkte mit sehr weißem Licht wählen, anstatt einer einzigen Lichtquelle für den gesamten Raum.

299

295

304

Quality and Quantity
Qualité et quantité
Qualität und Quantität

306

311

307

312

5 Colors give different results according to other colors around them.

Les couleurs changent leur effet sous l'influence des couleurs environnantes.

Die Wirkung der Farben ändert sich unter dem Einfluss der Farben in ihrer Umgebung.

6 Colors that lie opposite to each other on the color wheel give each other intensity. Red, for instance, looks redder next to green and green, in turn, looks more intense.

Les couleurs opposées au cercle chromatique s'intensifient entre elles. A titre d'exemple, le rouge semblera plus rouge à côté du vert et ce dernier, à son tour, gagnera en intensité.

Die Farben, die sich im Farbkreis gegenüberliegen, verstärken sich gegenseitig in ihrer Intensität. So wird Rot zum Beispiel noch intensiver, wenn es neben Grün zu sehen ist; ebenso wirkt die Farbe Grün stärker.

7 A pale color looks deeper next to a dark color than next to one of the same lightness.

Une couleur apparemment claire sera moins forte à côté d'une couleur foncée que si elle est à côté d'une autre aussi claire.

Eine helle Farbe wirkt stärker neben einer dunklen Farbe als neben einer Farbe der gleichen Helligkeitsstufe.

8 Quantity contrast refers to how surfaces of different sizes and colors interact with each other. A large single-color surface next to a small surface in a contrasting color will increase the visual impact of the larger surface.

Le contraste de quantité se réfère à l'impact des surfaces de différentes couleurs entre elles proportionnellement à leur taille. Une grande surface d'une couleur, à côté d'une petite de la couleur de contraste, augmente l'impact visuel de la surface principale.

Der Kontrast durch die Quantität bezieht sich auf die Größe, die Flächen in unterschiedlichen Farben im Vergleich zueinander haben. Eine große einfarbige Fläche neben einer kleinen Fläche in einer Kontrastfarbe erhöht die visuelle Wirkung der Hauptfläche.

309 So, to illustrate this, a display of yellow ceramic vases on a console will reinforce a strong blue-painted wall.

Ainsi par exemple, un mur peint en bleu intense aura plus d'impact avec une console décorée de vases de céramique de couleur jaune.

So kann man z. B. die Wirkung einer in starkem Blau gestrichenen Wand noch durch eine Konsole mit gelben Keramikkrügen erhöhen.

310 A warm color scheme needs a cold touch in order to appear balanced. This is the sort of effect created, for example, by green plants in ocher surroundings.

Un schéma de couleurs chaudes requiert une touche de couleur froide pour être équilibré. C'est l'effet produit par les plantes, par exemple, dans les espaces ocre.

Mehrere warme Farben benötigen als Ergänzung etwas kalte Farbe, damit das Gesamtbild ausgeglichen wirkt. Diese Wirkung können z. B. Pflanzen in einer ockerfarbenen Umgebung erzielen.

311 A cool area, on the other hand, needs a little warmth in order to become alive.

315

Par contre, une configuration froide nécessite l'impulsion d'un ton chaud pour reprendre vie.
Im Gegensatz dazu benötigt die Zusammenstellung kalter Farben auch ein Element in einem warmen Ton, um lebendiger zu wirken.

312 Strong colors should be reserved for small surfaces or to set off architectural elements such as columns, changes in floor level, or panels.
Il faut que les couleurs fortes s'appliquent sur des petites surfaces pour détacher des éléments architecturaux comme les colonnes, les différences de niveaux du sol ou les panneaux.
Starke Farben sollte man auf kleinen Flächen oder zum Betonen architektonischer Elemente wie Säulen, Höhenunterschiede des Bodens oder Paneele benutzen.

313 Pale shades are suitable for large surfaces.
Les couleurs claires sont adéquates pour les grandes surfaces.
Helle Farben eignen sich gut für große Flächen.

314 Combining too many colors can generate confusion and create a sensation of disorder.
Le mélange de nombreuses couleurs crée la confusion et communique un sentiment de désordre.
Die Mischung vieler verschiedener Farben wirkt sehr verwirrend und erweckt den Eindruck von Unordnung.

315 Pale cool shades appear lighter, while dark warm ones look heavier and more solid. This point must be taken into consideration in order to lessen the impact of large-sized furniture in small spaces.

Les tons froids et clairs paraissent plus légers, les chauds et fon semblent être plus lourds et denses. Gardant ceci à l'esprit, on p modifier, par exemple, l'impact de meubles très grands dans un esp réduit.
Kalte und helle Töne wirken leichter, warme und dunkle Töne dichter schwerer. Wenn man dies bedenkt, kann man z. B. die Wirkung gro Möbel in einem kleinen Raum mindern.

316 Neutral surroundings dominated by white, beige and pale gray nee few splashes of zesty color, which can be provided by simple eleme such as a few cushions laid out on a sofa.
Les ambiances neutres où le blanc, le beige ou le gris clair prédomin nécessitent des touches de couleur provenant de simples accessoi comme les coussins disposés sur le canapé.
Neutrale Räume, in denen Weiß, Beige oder Hellgrau vorherrsch benötigen Farbtupfer, die man z. B. durch einfache Elemente wie Kis auf einem Sofa schaffen kann.

Color and Ambience
Couleur et ambiance
Farbe und Ambiente

320

317 As a general rule, warm colors tend to make the walls in a room appear nearer. The opposite effect occurs whereby elements seem to recede when cool colors are used.

De règle générale, les couleurs chaudes ont tendance à rapprocher visuellement les murs. C'est juste le contraire qui se passe avec les éléments peints dans des couleurs froides : ils paraissent s'éloigner.

Als allgemeine Regel gilt, dass warme Farben die Wände visuell annähern. Genau das Gegenteil geschieht mit Elementen, die in kalten Farben gestrichen sind; sie scheinen weiter weg zu sein.

318 A long, narrow room will look shorter if the back wall is painted orange red and the side walls sage green.

Dans une chambre longue et étroite, on peut peindre le mur du fond en rouge corail et les côtés en vert sauge pour la raccourcir visuellement.

In einem langen und engen Raum kann man die hintere Wand Korallrot und die Seitenwände Salbeigrün streichen, um den Raum optisch kürzer zu machen.

319 This widening effect can also be achieved using various light and dark tones or different levels of saturation or intensity.

L'effet sur ce sentiment d'amplitude est également déterminé par les tons —clairs ou foncés— et l'intensité —saturation—.

Dieser visuelle Eindruck von Weite wird ebenso durch den Farbton (hell und dunkel) wie durch die Intensität oder Sättigung einer Farbe erweckt.

320 Both an intense green and the warmest of reds can also bring the walls closer, while a gentle yellow promotes a feeling of spaciousness by making them disappear.

Un vert intense ou bleu rapprochera également les murs de la m manière que le plus chaud des rouges, alors qu'un jaune très suave en sorte que les murs semblent s'effacer, accroissant ainsi le sentin d'espace.

Ein intensives Grün oder Blau nähert die Wände ebenfalls visuell an; Gleiche gilt für ein warmes Rot. Ein helles Gelb hingegen sorgt da dass die Wände sich aufzulösen scheinen, wodurch der Eindruck Weite verstärkt wird.

321 Dark flooring combined with pale walls and ceiling makes a room wider.

Un sol foncé aux murs et plafond de couleurs ou aux tons clairs, éla la chambre.

Ein dunkler Boden mit Wänden und Decke in hellen Farben und Tö lässt den Raum breiter wirken.

322 Dark flooring combined with a dark ceiling makes a room look wider brings its height down.

Un sol foncé, avec un plafond également foncé, élargit la chambr réduit la hauteur des murs.

Ein dunkler Boden mit einer dunklen Decke macht den Raum opt breiter und lässt die Wände niedriger wirken.

323 Dark walls in a room with a pale floor and ceiling set off horizontal li Des murs foncés, dans une chambre au sol et plafond de tons cl rehaussent les lignes horizontales.

Dunkle Wände in einem Raum mit einem hellen Boden und heller D betonen die horizontalen Linien.

Choosing a dark tint for the back wall of a room and light tones for the other walls and the floor will reduce its depth.
Un mur de fond foncé, des murs et un sol de couleurs ou de tons clairs, réduisent la profondeur de l'espace.
Eine dunkle Rückwand in Kombination mit den übrigen Wänden und einem Boden in hellen Farben und Tönen lassen den Raum optisch kürzer wirken.

A pale ceiling, with dark floors and walls will create a basement effect with the light concentrated only in the upper part of the room.
Un plafond clair avec un sol et des murs foncés, produit un effet d'attique où la lumière se concentre uniquement sur la partie supérieure.
Eine helle Decke mit dunklen Böden und Wänden lässt den Raum wie einen Keller wirken, in dem sich das Licht auf den oberen Teil konzentriert.

Light flooring and a pale back wall combined with dark side walls and ceiling will produce a tunnel effect.
Un sol clair avec un mur du fond également clair, des murs latéraux et un plafond foncés, créent un effet de tunnel.
Ein heller Boden mit einer ebenfalls hellen Rückwand und dunklen Seitenwänden und dunkler Decke erzeugt eine Tunnelwirkung.

The shapes of spaces in which the surfaces are all painted the same color tend to become blurred.
Les formes des espaces où la totalité des surfaces est peinte d'une même couleur, tendent à s'effacer.
Die Form eines Raumes, in dem alle Flächen in der gleichen Farbe gestrichen sind, scheint sich aufzulösen.

328 A room with pale flooring and walls creates the illusion of space.
Une chambre avec un sol et des murs clairs crée un sentiment d'espace.
Ein Raum mit einem hellen Boden und hellen Wänden wirkt sehr weit.

319

Continuity
Continuité
Kontinuität

339

329 As the rooms in small apartments tend to be quite close together, the harmony of the entire house depends on the colors chosen for each one of them.

Comme les chambres des petites habitations ont tendance à être très rapprochées, l'harmonie de toute la maison dépendra des couleurs qui s'appliquent à chacune d'elles.

Räume in kleinen Wohnungen liegen sehr nah beieinander und so hängt die Harmonie des Gesamtbildes von den jeweiligen Farben ab.

330 The use of unrelated colors in adjacent rooms makes the house look like an ensemble of separate and individual entities similar to that of many commercial spaces.

L'emploi de couleurs qui n'ont pas de lien chromatique dans des pièces voisines, fait que la maison est perçue comme un ensemble décousu, très similaire à celui de nombreux espaces commerciaux.

Die Verwendung von unterschiedlichen Farben in nebeneinander liegenden Zimmern lässt die Wohnung wie eine Folge unzusammenhängender Räume wirken, so wie dies oft bei kommerziell genutzten Lokalen der Fall ist.

331 Color is crucial for creating a pleasant atmosphere in studios of living spaces with large open areas, such as lofts, in which a single volume needs to be organized into various different activity zones.

Dans les chambres du type studio ou dans celles connectées à travers de grandes ouvertures, comme les lofts, il est encore plus important que les couleurs dégagent un sentiment de bien-être.

In Studiowohnungen oder Loftwohnungen, in denen die Räume durch große Öffnungen miteinander verbunden sind, ist es besonders wichtig, dass die Farben für einen angenehmen Eindruck sorgen.

332 Only two or three colors of different intensities and tones shoul used for a unifying effect.

Pour créer une unité, il faut limiter la palette à deux ou trois coul appliquées dans différentes intensités et tons.

Um ein einheitliches Gesamtbild zu erzielen, sollte man sich auf zwe drei Farben beschränken, die in verschiedenen Helligkeitsstufen Tönen benutzt werden können.

333 Using two colors that are next to each other on the color wheel guaranty fluidity between rooms.

Le choix des couleurs voisines dans le cercle chromatique garan fluidité des espaces.

Die Wahl von Farben, die im Farbkreis nebeneinander liegen, garar einen fließenden Übergang der Räume.

334 To separate an open kitchen from a family room, have the colors ch for the two areas meet on the partial wall or on the countertop.

Pour séparer les cuisines américaines du salon-salle à manger, il que la limite de couleurs entre les deux espaces de vie soit tirée à p du mur de partition ou du bar.

Um offene Küchen vom Wohn- und Speisezimmer abzutrennen, s man für die farbliche Begrenzung der beiden Bereiche einen Tei Wand oder die Bar wählen.

335 One way to separate two spaces while ensuring a smooth trans between them is to use the same color in different tones, reservin more intense tone for the space to be highlighted.

337

Pour différencier les deux espaces en douceur, recourir à la même couleur dans un dégradé de tons, gardant le plus intense pour l'ambiance que l'on veut faire ressortir.

Eine Methode, um beide Bereiche voneinander zu unterscheiden ist, die gleiche Farbe in verschiedenen Tönen zu verwenden, und dabei in dem Bereich, der visuell unterstrichen werden soll, die stärkere Farbe zu wählen.

6 If contrasting colors are to be used for two adjacent rooms, the floors should be the same color throughout in order to maintain continuity.

Si on veut peindre deux chambres contiguës de couleurs contrastées, la continuité se fera par une unité de couleur au sol.

Wenn man zwei nebeneinander liegende Räume in Kontrastfarben streichen möchte, kann man durch eine einheitliche Fußbodenfarbe Kontinuität schaffen.

7 Chromatic combinations need not be exactly the same in all the various rooms. Shades may be light or dark, as the eye will perceive the areas as being linked anyway.

Il n'est pas nécessaire que les associations chromatiques soient exactement les mêmes dans toutes les pièces. Les tons peuvent être légèrement plus clairs ou plus foncés, de toute manière, l'œil percevra la relation entre les espaces.

Es ist nicht notwendig, in allen Räumen exakt die gleiche Farbkombination zu benutzen. Auch wenn die Töne variieren, werden die Räume noch visuell miteinander in Verbindung stehen.

3 Another way of establishing continuity is to wallpaper the room that has the largest opening, using colors related to those of the other rooms.

Une autre façon d'instaurer cette continuité consiste à appliquer du papier peint sur la zone la plus ouverte de la maison, avec des couleurs en relation avec les autres pièces.

Eine andere Methode, um Kontinuität zu schaffen, ist, die offenere Räume in Farben zu tapezieren, die mit den anderen Zimmern in Verbindung stehen.

339 If white is the dominant color throughout the house, it should be combined with its own variants. For example, pure white for the sitting room, cream for bedrooms and bluish tones for the bathroom.

Si le blanc est la couleur prédominante dans toute la maison, on peut l'appliquer dans ses variantes diverses. Par exemple : pur pour le salon, crème pour les chambres à coucher et avec des tons bleutés pour la salle de bains.

Wenn Weiß die vorherrschende Farbe im ganzen Haus ist, kann man es in verschiedenen Tönen verwenden. Zum Beispiel ein reines Weiß für das Wohnzimmer, Creme in den Schlafzimmern und ein bläuliches Weiß im Bad.

340 To determine where fields of color should begin and end in large open spaces, such as lofts, it is necessary to start with the areas as defined by furniture groupings and then go from there.

Pour définir où commence et s'achève une couleur dans les chambres très ouvertes, comme les lofts, il suffit de partir des ambiances créées par le mobilier pour peindre ensuite les murs.

Um zu definieren, wo eine Farbe in einer sehr offenen Wohnung wie z. B. in einem Loft beginnt und wo sie endet, sollte man von der Raumteilung ausgehen, die durch die Möbel entsteht, und darauf basierend die Wände streichen.

Styles
Styles
Stile

352

351

347

346

1 Off-white and matt pastels are the most characteristic colors of Provençal decoration. More contemporary versions include greens, terracottas, blues and deep reds.

La décoration provençale se reconnaît par la prédominance du blanc ivoire et des tons pastel mates. Les versions les plus modernes intègrent des rouges profonds, verts, terre cuite et bleus.

Typisch für die Dekoration im provenzalischen Stil ist die Verwendung der Farbe Eierschale und von matten Pastelltönen. Die modernen Versionen schließen auch ein tiefes Rot, Grün, Terrakotta und Blautöne ein.

2 Rustic styles use earth colors in combination with fur throws and animal skin rugs, leather upholstered furniture and accessories. Adding orange red and intense green makes for an African style decor.

Les styles rustiques emploient les tons de terre, associés à des jetés et tapis en peau d'animal et meubles en cuir et accessoires. En ajoutant le rouge corail et le vert intense, le style se transforme et prend un air africain.

In den rustikalen Stilrichtungen verwendet man Erdtöne in Kombination mit Decken und Teppichen aus Tierfell und mit Ledermöbeln und Dekorationselementen. Wenn man dazu Korallrot oder ein intensives Grün kombiniert, verändert sich die Umgebung und bekommt einen afrikanischen Touch.

3 Pale wood furniture and white are the most vital elements in northern European and Scandinavian decoration.

La décoration scandinave ou nordique, se nourrit de bois aux tons clairs, associé au blanc.

Die skandinavische oder nordische Dekoration beruht auf Holz in hellen Tönen in Kombination mit Weiß.

344 Houses with a more traditional decor feature peach, olive green, chocolate brown and aubergine tints with a matt finish.

Les maisons de décoration plus classiques ou traditionnelles ont recours aux tons pêche, vert olive, marron chocolat et aubergine avec des finitions mates.

In Häusern mit einer klassischeren oder traditionellen Dekoration benutzt man Töne wie Pfirsich, Olivgrün, Schokoladenbraun und Aubergine in matter Ausführung.

345 Contemporary decoration includes a palette of whites, blue-greens and blues, as well as bright red and orange, mixing degrees of glossiness and textures.

La décoration contemporaine décline une palette de blancs, verts bleutés et bleus, tels le rouge vif et l'orange, métissés de scintillements et de textures.

In der zeitgenössischen Innenarchitektur verwendet man eine Reihe von Weißtönen, Blaugrün- und Blautönen, ebenso starkes Rot und Orange, wobei man Glanz und Texturen variiert.

346 Minimalist styles focus around white, gray and beige as the basic colors.

Les styles minimalistes ont recours au blanc, gris, noir et beige comme couleurs principales.

Die minimalistischen Stilrichtungen sind von den Farben Weiß, Grau, Schwarz, Beige und den Grundfarben geprägt.

343

347 Zen Japanese interiors feature combinations of black and white with natural wood, while Chinese decoration favors blacks with reds.
La décoration zen japonaise utilise le blanc, le bois et el noir, alors qu'en
Chine c'est l'association rouge et noir qui prédomine.
Im japanischen Zen-Stil werden schwarz-weiße Kombinationen verwendet und Holz, während in China die Kombination von Rot mit Schwarz
vorherrscht.

348 The combination of reds, oranges, pinks and magentas is particular to
Indian style environments.
L'association de rouge, orange, rose et magenta est la favorite des
atmosphères de style indien.
Die Kombination von Rot-, Orange-, Rosa- und Magentatönen ist in
Wohnumgebungen im indischen Stil sehr beliebt.

349 The 'industrial' look involves metallic finishes combined with blue, gray
and brown.
Le *look* industriel utilise les finitions métalliques, associées au bleu, gris
et marron.
Um einen industriellen Look zu erzielen, werden gerne metallische Flächen in Kombination mit Blau, Grau und Braun verwendet.

350 Turquoise, white, orange and brown are the most characteristic colors of
1970s retro styles.
Turquoise, blanc, orange et marron sont de mise dans les styles rétro
des années soixante-dix.
Türkis, Weiß, Orange und Braun sind die Lieblingsfarben des Retrostils
der Siebzigerjahre.

351 Primary colors are ideal for 'pop' styles.
Les couleurs primaires sont idéales pour les ambiances d'inspiration
Die Primärfarben eignen sich ausgezeichnet für Räume, die sich an
Pop-Art inspirieren.

352 Intense colors in combination with curvilinear furniture and glass ac
sories are the signature components of neobaroque decoration.
Le néo-baroque favorise les couleurs intenses associées à des meu
aux formes courbes et accessoires de verre.
Der neobarocke Stil kombiniert intensive Farben mit geschwunge
Formen und Dekorationselementen aus Glas und Kristall.

Hallways Entrées Eingangsbereiche
Corridors and Staircases Couloirs et
escaliers Flure und Treppen
Dining Rooms Salles à manger
Speisezimmer Living Rooms Salons
Wohnzimmer Bedrooms Chambres
à coucher Schlafzimmer Kitchens
Cuisines Küchen Bathrooms Salles
de bains Badezimmer Children's
Rooms Chambres d'enfants
Kinderzimmer Work Areas Zones
de travail Arbeitsbereiche Patios
and Terraces Patios et terrasses
Höfe und Terrassen Decorative
Elements Éléments décoratifs

Color and Spaces
Couleur et espaces
Farbe und Räume

The functions of each of the rooms in a house usually determine the type of furniture, space arrangement and decoration it requires. However, bearing in mind the great influence color has on moods, choosing the right tint is very important when trying to inject dynamism and energy into the most active rooms, for example, or to induce relaxation in areas meant for sleep and rest. For this reason, working out the correct chromatic configuration for each living space is a crucial factor for the mental well-being of its occupants.

Les fonctions de chacune des pièces de l'habitation définissent le type de mobilier, le design de l'espace et sa décoration. Mais de par la grande influence exercée par la couleur sur les états d'âme, elle joue un rôle fondamental à l'heure de favoriser, par exemple, le dynamisme et l'énergie dans les chambres les plus actives, ou d'inciter à la relaxation et au calme dans celles qui sont destinées au repos. C'est pour cela, que l'art de résoudre la configuration chromatique de chaque espace sera pour le moins déterminant, sur la qualité de vie des habitants de la maison.

Die Funktion eines jedes Raumes in einer Wohnung oder einem Haus definiert die Art der Möbel, die Gestaltung und die Dekoration. Da Farben jedoch einen großen Einfluss auf die Stimmung des Menschen haben, spielen sie eine grundlegende Rolle, wenn man zum Beispiel die Dynamik und die Energie in häufig genutzten Räumen verstärken oder in den Ruheräumen eine entspannte und ruhige Atmosphäre schaffen möchte. Deshalb bestimmt die farbliche Gestaltung der verschiedenen Räume entscheidend die Lebensqualität ihrer Bewohner.

453

423

Hallways
Entrées
Eingangsbereiche

353

353 The entry hall is the introductory component of a house. It must therefore be consistent with the style and color range used in the rest of the house.
Le vestibule est la carte de visite de la maison. Pour ce faire, il doit être en harmonie avec le style et la gamme de couleurs du reste de l'habitation.
Der Eingangsbereich ist die Visitenkarte eines jeden Hauses. Deshalb sollte man bei dessen Gestaltung einen stilistischen Zusammenhang mit den im Rest der Wohnung verwendeten Farben suchen.

354 If the house is small, the entry hall should try to convey a feeling of space. Light colored walls will help achieve this effect.
Si la maison est petite, l'entrée devra transmette une sensation d'espace. Pour ce faire, appliquer des peintures claires sur les murs.
Wenn die Wohnung klein ist, sollte der Eingangsbereich den Eindruck von Weite erwecken. Dieser Eindruck kann durch die Verwendung heller Farben an den Wänden geschaffen werden.

355 Another option is to paint the wall opposite the front door one particular color and leave the other walls white.
Une autre option consiste à peindre le mur opposé à la porte d'une couleur et laisser le reste en blanc.
Eine andere Möglichkeit ist, die Wand, die der Tür gegenüberliegt, in einer bestimmten Farbe zu streichen, und die übrigen in Weiß.

356 Pure colors or strong tints can be used if the entry is spacious and bright.
Si l'entrée est spacieuse et claire, on utilisera des couleurs plus pures, aux nuances plus fortes.
Wenn der Eingangsbereich weit und hell ist, kann man reinere Farben und stärkere Nuancen benutzen.

357 If the entry is not self-contained but leads directly to a sitting room small amount of wall surface can be 'appropriated' from that room painted a harmonious color.
Si la maison ne dispose pas d'un espace indépendant pour l'entrée, peindra une petite surface du mur du salon d'une couleur harmonieu
Wenn es in der Wohnung keinen unabhängigen Eingangsbereich g kann man der Wohnzimmerwand einen kleinen Teil der Fläche „raub und sie in einer harmonischen Farbe streichen.

358 Getting rid of any color contrast between the walls and the wainscott or baseboards visually enlarges the available space.
Eliminer le contraste entre la couleur des murs et les frises ou soc permet d'agrandir visuellement l'espace.
Auch der Verzicht auf einen Kontrast zwischen der Wandfarbe und Friesen und Sockeln macht den Raum optisch größer.

359 Walls divided horizontally appear wider. A darker tone should be used ground the lower part.
La division horizontale des murs élargit visuellement ces surfaces convient de rehausser la partie inférieure avec un ton plus foncé que partie supérieure.
Die horizontale Teilung der Wände macht die entsprechende Fläc optisch größer. Man sollte den unteren Teil mit einer dunkleren Far hervorheben.

360 Transparent acrylic or silver-painted wooden consoles create the illus of using up very little space.

Les consoles de méthacrylate transparent ou de bois peint en argent occupent visuellement très peu d'espace.
Konsolen aus transparentem Metakrylat oder silbern gestrichenem Holz nehmen visuell wenig Platz ein.

1 Light fixtures that produce a white light are the best choice for the entry. Colored lighting should be left for other spaces.
À l'entrée, il est conseillé d'installer des ampoules qui émettent une lumière blanche et de réserver l'éclairage coloré pour d'autres espaces.
Es ist empfehlenswert, im Eingangsbereich Glühbirnen zu verwenden, die weißes Licht ausstrahlen, und bunte Beleuchtung in anderen Räumen zu verwenden.

2 Hatstands take up more space than wall-mounted coat racks. However, painting them a paler color than the wall helps them lose some of their heaviness.
Les portemanteaux sur pied occupent plus d'espace que ceux qui sont suspendus, bien que peints dans un ton plus clair que le mur, ils acquièrent une certaine légèreté visuelle.
Garderobenständer nehmen an der Wand mehr Platz weg als Kleiderhaken. Wenn man sie jedoch in einer helleren Farbe als die Wand streicht, wirken sie optisch leichter.

3 If there is enough room for a narrow wardrobe, the best color for it is one close to that of the walls on the chromatic wheel.
S'il y a de la place pour une armoire étroite, il vaut mieux qu'elle soit d'une couleur voisine, dans le cercle chromatique, à celle des murs.

Falls Platz für einen schmalen Schrank vorhanden ist, sollte er eine Farbe haben, die im Farbkreis in der Nähe der Wandfarbe liegt.

364 Rooms that receive little sunlight appear a lot smaller. A yellow tint is the most appropiate for achieving the effect of natural light in an entry.
Les pièces peu lumineuses paraissent beaucoup trop petites. Pour créer dans l'entrée un effet de lumière naturelle, on peut recourir à la gamme de jaune.
Dunkle Räume wirken viel kleiner. Um im Eingangsbereich die Wirkung von Tageslicht zu verstärken, kann man auf gelbe Farben zurückgreifen.

365 Wallpaper with silver motifs on a white background makes the walls look larger and create such visual impact that no furniture is required.
Les papiers peints avec fond blanc et motifs argent agrandissent visuellement les murs et créent un impact visuel tel, qu'il n'est pas nécessaire d'y installer des meubles.
Tapeten mit einem weißen Hintergrund und silbernen Motiven machen die Wände optisch größer und haben eine so starke visuelle Wirkung, dass man auf Möbel verzichten kann.

366 An alternative to the traditional hall mirror is a large picture or poster on the main wall. Either item should be paler than the actual wall.
Un grand cadre ou poster accroché sur la surface principale de l'entrée, remplacera un miroir classique. Les choisir dans des tons plus clairs que le mur qui les accueille.
Eine Alternative zum klassischen Spiegel ist ein großes Bild oder Poster auf der Hauptwand im Eingangsbereich. Es sollte hellere Farben als die Wand haben, an der es hängt.

357

Corridors and Staircases
Couloirs et escaliers
Flure und Treppen

368

367 To make a corridor look wider, the side walls should be painted a light
color and the facing walls a dark one.
Pour élargir visuellement un couloir, il faut peindre de couleur claire les
murs latéraux et en couleur foncée les murs frontaux.
Um einen Flur visuell zu vergrößern, sollte man die Seitenwände in einer
hellen Farbe und die vorderen Wände dunkel streichen.

368 A pale floor makes walls appear more distant.
Un sol de couleur claire permet d'éloigner les murs.
Ein heller Boden lässt die Wände weiter entfernt wirken.

369 Light-colored walls combined with a darker floor and ceiling make a corridor look shorter.
Pour couper la longueur d'un couloir, appliquer sur les murs un ton clair
et peindre plafond et sol d'une teinte plus foncée.
Wenn ein Flur optisch verkürzt werden soll, kann man die Wände hell
und die Decke sowie den Boden etwas dunkler gestalten.

370 Heavily used areas can appear shorter if they are decorated with hori-
zontally striped rugs in complementary colors.
Les tapis aux rayures horizontales de couleurs complémentaires, rédui-
sent la longueur des aires de passage.
Teppiche mit horizontalen Streifen in Komplementärfarben machen die
Durchgangsbereiche kürzer.

371 If the stripe pattern of the rug only involves one color and its various
graded hues it will give more depth to the space.

Si au contraire les couleurs des rayures reflètent un dégradé de différ
tes tonalités d'une même couleur, le tapis donne de la profondeur à l
pace.
Wenn im Gegensatz dazu die Farben der Streifen in verschiede
Tönen einer einzigen Farbe fortgesetzt werden, verleiht der Teppich d
Raum Tiefe.

372 Baseboards painted the same color as the floor make staircases a
corridors look wider.
Les socles de bois peints de la même couleur que le sol élargissent
escaliers ou les couloirs.
Holzsockel in der gleichen Farbe wie der Fußboden lassen Treppen
Flure optisch breiter wirken.

373 When the top part of a wall is painted a darker color than the rest, v
lamps should be mounted the whole length of the corridor.
Lorsque la frange supérieure du mur est dans un ton plus foncé que l
férieur, il faut installer des appliques de lumière tout au long du coul
Wenn der obere Teil einer Wand dunkler als der untere ist, sollte man
gesamten Flur Wandlampen anbringen.

374 Walking up stairs seems less of a chore if the walls of the landing at
top of the staircase are painted a warm color.
Peindre en tons chauds le mur du palier de l'escalier, diminue la sen
tion de fatigue.
Wenn man die Wand an den Treppenabsätzen in einer warmen Fa
streicht, erscheint der Aufstieg müheloser.

369

379

Transparent stairs tend to disappear against their surroundings and are therefore ideal for very small spaces.
Les escaliers transparents tendent à se fondre dans l'environnement : ils sont donc idéals pour les très petits espaces.
Transparente Treppen scheinen mit der Umgebung zu verschmelzen, deshalb eignen sie sich ausgezeichnet für kleine Räume.

Another possibility is to paint the steps and banisters the same as the predominant color of the house, or a lighter shade.
Peindre les marches et la rambarde de la même couleur ou dans un ton plus clair que le ton dominant de la pièce, est une autre possibilité.
Eine andere Möglichkeit ist, die Stufen und Geländer in der gleichen Farbe oder in einem helleren Ton als dem zu streichen, der im Raum vorherrscht.

A metallic staircase with yellow steps and a white banister will liven up very open, neutral dominated environments.
Un escalier métallique aux marches peintes en jaune avec des rambardes blanches met de la vie dans les ambiances très ouvertes, dominées par les tons neutres.
Eine Metalltreppe mit gelben Stufen und weißem Geländer verleihen sehr offenen Räumen, in denen neutrale Töne vorherrschen, mehr Leben.

A staircase wall painted in a primary color and lit with pin spotlights will look quite dramatic.
Les points de lumière installés le long des marches, contre un mur d'une couleur primaire, créent un effet théâtral.

Eine theatralische Wirkung erzielt man, indem man die Wand in einer Primärfarbe streicht und entlang der Stufen Strahler anbringt.

379 To give a wood stair an unusual touch, paint it with a 'trompe l'oeil' carpet, either as a runner down the center of the steps or completely covering it.
Pour donner une touche d'originalité à un escalier en bois, on peut peindre un tapis en *trompe l'œil* qui occupe la zone centrale le long des marches.
Um eine Holztreppe originell zu gestalten, kann man ein *trompe l'œil* malen, mit dem ein Teppich auf den Stufen vorgetäuscht wird.

380 Painting the steps of uneven staircases a complementary color to that of the house will enhance them and turn them into a supporting decorative accessory.
Pour faire ressortir les marches des escaliers entre deux niveaux, et les transformer en support d'accessoires décoratifs, les peindre d'une couleur complémentaire à celle de la pièce.
Um die Stufen einer Treppe zwischen zwei Ebenen hervorzuheben, kann man sie in einer Komplementärfarbe zur Raumefarbe streichen. Die Stufen werden so zu einem weileren dekorativen Detail.

376

Dining Rooms
Salles à manger
Speisezimmer

394

382

393

Primary colors, combined with those next to them on the chromatic wheel, go quite well in the dining room, a dynamic space in the house.

Dans la salle à manger, zone très dynamique de la maison, les couleurs primaires, combinées à leurs voisines, dans le cercle chromatique sont idéales.

Im Speisezimmer, einem der dynamischsten Räume der Wohnung, kann man gut Primärfarben in Kombination mit benachbarten Farben im Farbkreis verwenden.

The contrast between white walls and colored furniture brings freshness to the house.

Le contraste entre les murs blancs et les meubles de couleur apporte fraîcheur à la pièce.

Der Kontrast zwischen den weißen Wänden und den bunten Möbeln lässt den Raum frisch wirken.

When the wall is the brightly colored element, however, the furniture should be white or pale wood.

Si, au contraire, c'est le mur qui affiche la couleur intense, choisir des meubles blancs ou en bois clair.

Wenn die Wand jedoch eine intensive Farbe hat, sollten die Möbel Weiß oder aus hellem Holz sein.

To set each other off, the living room and the dining room should be painted the same color but in different shades.

Pour séparer le salon de la salle à manger, peindre les murs de ces espaces dans un ton de la même couleur.

Um das Wohnzimmer vom Speisezimmer abzutrennen, kann man die Wände dieser Bereiche in zwei verschiedenen Tönen der gleichen Farbe streichen.

385 The dining room needs one reliable light. A lamp of the same tone as the table and mounted above it will be enough.

La salle à manger nécessite une lumière ponctuelle. Une lampe du même ton que la table au-dessus de laquelle elle est placée, sera suffisante.

Für das Speisezimmer empfiehlt sich ein Lichtpunkt. Dabei reicht eine Lampe über dem Tisch aus, die den gleichen Farbton wie dieser hat.

386 Low, pale-colored cabinets or sideboards are ideal for providing useful storage space for tableware while maintaining a feeling of spaciousness.

Pour gagner de l'espace, le mieux est que la vaisselle soit rangée dans des meubles bas aux tons clairs.

Um den Raum größer wirken zu lassen, sollte man das Geschirr in niedrigen Möbeln in hellen Farben aufbewahren.

387 When an extendable dining table is used, a bench along the wall can be an invaluable space-saving element. Use it in combination with chairs of the same color on the other side of the table.

Si la table est allongée, pour gagner de l'espace, placer un banc contre le mur et les sièges de l'autre côté (tous de la même couleur).

Wenn der Tisch eine längliche Form hat, kann man Platz gewinnen, indem man eine Bank an die Wandseite und Stühle auf die andere Seite stellt; alle in der gleichen Farbe.

390

388 If the dining room also serves as an office, its decoration should feature the same range of colors as the kitchen.

Si la salle à manger fait partie d'un *office*, ce dernier devra afficher la même gamme de couleurs que la cuisine.

Wenn das Speisezimmer zur offenen Küche gehört, sollte es in den gleichen Farben wie die Küche gestaltet sein.

389 Glass and brushed- or chromed-steel furniture are the most suitable for dining rooms that get very little natural light.

Les meubles en verre et acier mat ou chromés sont les plus appropriés pour les salles à manger bénéficiant de peu de lumière naturelle.

Für Essbereiche mit wenig Tageslicht eignen sich ausgezeichnet Möbel aus Glas oder mattem oder verchromtem Stahl.

390 When choosing the color for the walls, the best way to establish a harmonious composition is to start with the furniture.

Pour choisir la couleur des murs, on partira du mobilier pour créer une association de couleurs harmonieuse.

Um die Farbe der Wände zu wählen, sollte man von den Möbeln ausgehen und eine harmonische Farbkomposition schaffen.

391 An ocher-colored table and orange chairs, for example, suggest yellow as the ideal tone for the walls.

Ainsi, par exemple, une table de couleur ocre et des sièges orange imposent le jaune comme le ton approprié pour les murs.

Wenn der Tisch z. B. ockerfarben ist und die Stühle Orange, bietet sich für die Wände Gelb an.

392 Black upholstered armchairs absorb a large quantity of light and ap to take up less room as a result.

Les fauteuils recouverts de toile de couleur noire absorbent beauco lumière et paraissent occuper moins d'espace.

Mit schwarzem Stoff bezogene Sessel verschlucken viel Licht und se nen weniger Raum einzunehmen.

393 Round colorful rugs contrasting with the floor help define the d room area.

Les tapis ronds, d'une couleur qui contraste avec celle du sol, per tent de délimiter l'espace de la salle à manger.

Runde, einfarbige Teppiche, im Kontrast zum Fußboden, dienen Begrenzung des Essbereiches.

394 The pure sharp lines of minimalist dining rooms are enhanced by predominance of black and white.

Les lignes pures et contondantes des salles à manger minimalistes renforcées par la prédominance du blanc et noir.

Klare und kräftige Linien in minimalistisch gestalteten Speisezimr werden durch die Farben Schwarz und Weiß unterstrichen.

386

Living Rooms
Salons
Wohnzimmer

404

395 As the living room is meant for social gatherings, entertainment and relaxation, it should be harmonious and, above all, welcoming.

Le salon étant un lieu de rencontre, distraction et détente, il est essentiel qu'il offre un aspect harmonieux et, surtout, accueillant.

Da das Wohnzimmer der Raum des Zusammentreffens, der Unterhaltung und Entspannung ist, sollte es harmonisch und vor allem gemütlich sein.

396 A living room in which a warm color scheme dominates needs a cool element – a green or a lilac armchair – for the right balance.

Un salon où domine un schéma de couleurs chaudes nécessite une touche de couleur froide — un fauteuil vert ou lilas — pour qu'il soit équilibré.

In ein Wohnzimmer, in dem warme Farben dominieren, sollte man auch etwas kalte Farbe bringen, z. B. einen grünen oder violetten Sessel, um ein Gleichgewicht zu schaffen.

397 If the living room is composed of cool tones, it needs a warm-colored object – a lamp or a side table – to give it life.

Si le salon est composé de tons froids, il suffit de l'agrémenter d'un objet de couleur chaude, une lampe ou une table d'appoint, pour qu'il reprenne vie.

Wenn das Wohnzimmer in kalten Farben gestaltet ist, sollte die Dekoration durch ein Objekt in einer warmen Farbe ergänzt werden, um Leben hineinzubringen. Das kann eine Lampe oder ein Beistelltisch sein.

398 Mustard colored walls give brightness to a living room that gets very little natural light. Off-white sofas and curtains create an illusion of spaciousness.

Le ton moutarde des murs illumine les salons peu éclairés. Les cana et rideaux de couleur ivoire agrandissent l'espace.

Senffarbene Wände machen Wohnzimmer, in die wenig Tageslicht f heller. Eierschalenfarbene Sofas und Gardinen schaffen mehr Weite.

399 The use of green in living rooms that open out onto a patio or a terr where there are a lot of plants helps integrate the interior with the exte

L'emploi du vert dans les salons qui donnent sur un patio ou une rasse avec beaucoup de plantes permet de créer une ambiance qui s tègre à l'extérieur.

Die Farbe Grün in Wohnzimmern, die zu einem Innenhof oder einer rasse mit vielen Pflanzen liegen, trägt dazu bei, den Innen- mit d Außenraum zu verbinden.

400 Being a neutral color, charcoal gray makes a wide range of combinat possible. Warm colors are its best allies in the decoration of liv rooms.

Couleur neutre, le gris anthracite permet une large gamme d'asso tions de couleurs. Dans les salons, les couleurs chaudes sont son m leur allié.

Anthrazitgrau ist eine neutrale Farbe, die viele Kombinationen zulä Im Wohnzimmer kann man Anthrazitgrau gut mit warmen Farben kon nieren.

401 Rugs with geometrical patterns in the same color range give minima living rooms a modern style.

Les tapis aux motifs géométriques dans la même gamme de coul confèrent un style moderne aux salons minimalistes.

395

Teppiche mit geometrischen Motiven innerhalb der gleichen Farbskala lassen minimalistische Wohnzimmer sehr modern wirken.

2 A gold colored coffee table combined with black, gray and beige furnishings helps create a contemporary atmosphere.
Les tables de milieu de couleur or génèrent des ambiances contemporaines dans les salons au mobilier noir, gris et beige.
Goldene Couchtische lassen Wohnzimmer mit schwarzen, grauen und beigen Möbeln sehr zeitgemäß wirken.

3 Red leather sofas provide great contrast with the concrete floor finish of industrial interiors.
Les canapés en cuir rouge se marient, par contraste, avec les ambiances de type industriel aux finitions de béton.
Rote Ledersofas bilden einen schönen Kontrast in industriell wirkenden Wohnumgebungen mit viel Beton.

4 Multicolored rugs are suitable for living rooms with all-white surfaces and furniture.
Les tapis très colorés sont uniquement valables pour les salons où toutes les surfaces et les meubles sont blancs.
Bunte Teppiche eignen sich nur für Wohnzimmer, in denen alle Flächen weiß sind.

5 Overcrowding a small living room can be avoided by choosing low, horizontal furniture in a lighter tone than the walls.
Pour ne pas charger un petit salon, il est conseillé d'opter pour des meubles bas et horizontaux, aux tons plus clairs que les murs.

Um ein kleines Wohnzimmer nicht zu überladen, kann man niedrige und waagerechte Möbel in Farben, die heller als die der Wände sind, wählen.

406 Built-in sitting areas of brick or stone suit small spaces very well and provide endless possibilities for foam-filled seats and back cushions.
Les canapés en dur s'adaptent très bien aux petits espaces et permettent de jouer avec les couleurs du couvre-lit, des coussins et du dossier.
Gepolsterte Sofas passen gut in kleine Räume. Man kann mit den Farben des Bezugs und der Kissen spielen.

407 Wallpapers with a fine pattern contribute to a more spacious environment.
Les papiers peints aux petits motifs agrandissent l'univers.
Tapeten mit kleinen Motiven lassen den Raum größer wirken.

408 Fabrics with a floral pattern or large pictures tend to make living rooms look smaller, so they are best avoided in upholstery or curtains.
Les imprimés fleuris ou les grands carrés réduisent visuellement le salon; il est donc déconseillé de les utiliser pour les murs ou les rideaux.
Blumendrucke oder ein großes Karomuster reduzieren das Wohnzimmer optisch, deshalb sollte man diese Drucke an den Bezügen und Gardinen vermeiden.

405

402

398

400

Bedrooms
Chambres à coucher
Schlafzimmer

417

409 Cool colors like blue, green and violet impart calm and tranquillity. For this reason they are the most popular colors chosen for bedrooms.
Les couleurs froides, comme le bleu, vert et violet, diffusant calme et tranquillité, sont les favorites des chambres à coucher.
Kalte Farben wie Blau, Grün und Violett vermitteln Ruhe und Gelassenheit, deshalb wählt man sie oft für Schlafzimmer.

410 The combination of pale-gray walls and an intense-blue bedspread is not only elegant but also brightens up the room.
Le gris clair sur les murs et le bleu intense sur le lit forment une association de couleurs toute en élégance qui, de surcroît, illumine l'espace.
Das Hellgrau der Wände und das intensive Blau des Bettes bilden eine elegante Kombination, die außerdem noch Licht in den Raum bringt.

411 Harmonious color combinations induce relaxation, but there are no set rules for choosing the right colors.
Ajoutons que les associations harmonieuses sont relaxantes. Mais, à l'heure de choisir la couleur d'une chambre à coucher, il n'y a pas de règles fixes.
Auch die harmonischen Kombinationen wirken entspannend. Aber es gibt keine festen Regeln für die Farbauswahl im Schlafzimmer.

412 Printed fabrics and paints can co-exist happily as long as they belong to the same color range.
Les imprimés sont acceptables, s'ils gardent la même gamme de couleurs.
Ebenso können verschiedene Drucke miteinander kombiniert werden, wenn sie in der gleichen Farbskala liegen.

413 Pastel shades generate spaciousness. Contrasted with darker elemer they provide greater visual depth.
Les tons pastel donnent un sentiment d'amplitude. Il est important d troduire un contraste avec des éléments plus foncés pour obtenir profondeur visuelle.
Pastelltöne lassen den Raum weiter wirken. Sie sollten mit dunkle Elementen kombiniert werden, um eine visuelle Tiefe zu schaffen.

414 As a substitute for a headboard, a specific stretch of wall by the to the bed can be painted a lighter tint than the rest of the wall.
Pour remplacer la tête de lit, il suffit de peindre à sa place un esp donné, d'une couleur plus claire que celle du mur.
Wenn man auf das Kopfteil des Bettes verzichten möchte, sc man einen Teil der Wand am Kopfende in einer etwas helleren Fa streichen.

415 A standing wardrobe will not be so obvious in the room if finished in ural wood or painted to match the walls.
Une armoire en bois naturel, ou dans le même ton que les murs, se blera prendre moins de place.
Ein Schrank aus hellem Holz oder in der gleichen Farbe wie die W scheint weniger Platz wegzunehmen.

416 Oak, beech or maple flooring bring warmth to overly dark bedrooms.
Les parquets en chêne, hêtre ou érable ajoutent de la chaleur à chambre à coucher sombre.
Fußböden aus Eiche, Buche oder Ahorn lassen ein düsteres Schlafz mer wärmer wirken.

410

414

17 If there is not enough room for bedside tables, a shelf or a ledge (in the same color as the wall) can be built above the head of the bed.

S'il n'y a pas de place pour les tables de nuit, on peut placer une poutre ou un muret en maçonnerie (de la même couleur que le mur) sur la tête de lit.

Wenn kein Platz für Nachttische vorhanden ist, kann man ein Regalbrett oder eine kleine Mauer (in der gleichen Farbe wie die Wand) über dem Kopfteil des Bettes anbringen.

18 A trunk at the foot of the bed provides storage space and can even be used as a small bench.

Placés au pied du lit, les coffres servent de rangement, de tables ou même de siège.

In den Truhen am Fußende des Bettes kann man Dinge aufbewahren. Gleichzeitig dienen sie als Tische oder sogar als Bänke.

19 To provide intimacy in a bedroom with very high ceilings, paint the ceiling a slightly deeper shade than the walls.

Pour donner de la chaleur aux chambres à coucher aux plafonds très hauts, il suffit de peindre le faux plafond d'un ton légèrement plus foncé que les murs.

Um Schlafzimmer mit hohen Decken wärmer wirken zu lassen, sollte man die Zimmerdecke etwas dunkler als die Wände streichen.

20 Storage boxes built into the lower part of the bed must be of a neutral color if they are to remain unobtrusive.

Les tiroirs, qui optimalisent l'espace situé sous le lit, doivent avoir une couleur neutre pour passer inaperçus.

Die Schubladen, die unter dem Bett platzsparend angebracht sind, sollten eine neutrale Farbe haben, damit sie nicht auffallen.

421 In attic bedrooms the short pony walls should all be painted the same color.

Les murs des chambres à coucher qui, situés dans la mansarde, ont des plafonds inclinés, doivent être peints de la même couleur.

Die Lampen in Schlafzimmern mit geneigten Decken sollten die Farbe der Decke haben.

422 Pictures hung on either side of the bed, rather than just above it, give a greater feeling of spaciousness.

Situés à côté du lit, les cadres agrandissent davantage l'espace que lorsqu'ils sont situés au-dessus de la tête de lit.

Wenn man Bilder auf beiden Seiten des Bettes statt am Kopfende aufhängt, wirkt der Raum größer.

409

416

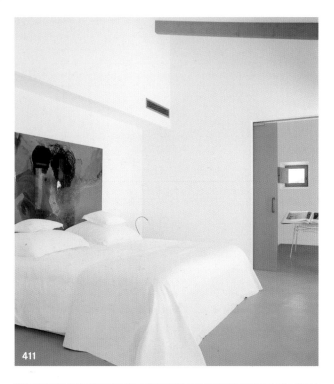

411

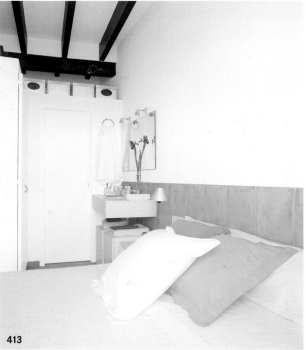

413

Kitchens
Cuisines
Küchen

429

423 Intense colors are suitable even for small kitchens thanks to the light reflected by metallic or glossy materials.
Même petites, les cuisines supportent des couleurs intenses grâce à la lumière qu'apportent les matériaux aux finitions métalliques et brillantes.
Auch in kleinen Küchen kann man starke Farben verwenden, da es Materialien mit glänzenden oder metallischen Flächen gibt, die mehr Licht in den Raum bringen.

424 Halogen lighting renders food in its true colors. So it's perfect for food-handling areas.
L'éclairage halogène ne modifie pas les couleurs. Il est donc idéal dans la zone de la cuisine où l'on manipule les aliments.
Halogenleuchten verändern die Farben nicht. Deshalb eignen sie sich besonders gut für die Bereiche der Küche, in denen man mit Lebensmitteln umgeht.

425 Slate clad walls give a contemporary look to kitchens with lacquered, red and acid-green laminate furnishings.
Les murs revêtus d'ardoise confèrent un air moderne aux cuisines dotées de mobilier rouge ou vert acidulé, aux laminés brillants.
Mit Schiefer verkleidete Wände lassen Küchen mit rot oder grün glänzenden Möbeln sehr modern wirken.

426 Orange and yellow, colors that bring light, combine well with cupboards that have a natural wood finish.
L'orange et le jaune, couleurs lumineuses, se marient avec les armoires aux finitions en bois.

Orange und Gelb sind Farben, die Licht in den Raum bringen. Sie pass gut zu Holzmöbeln.

427 Thanks to new materials that include quartz and resin, worktops come smooth, intense colors.
Grâce aux nouveaux matériaux, associant quartz et résine, les plans travail affichent des couleurs lisses et intenses.
Mit neuen Materialien, die Quarz und Kunstharz kombinieren, kann m Arbeitsflächen in vollen und intensiven Farben schaffen.

428 To achieve a feeling of spaciousness there should be only two domin colors in a kitchen, other than the metallic finish of countertops or fixtur
Pour donner le sentiment d'espace, il ne doit y avoir que deux coule dominantes (sans compter avec l'argent des plans de travail, etc.).
Um einen Raum optisch zu vergrößern, sollte er nur in zwei Farben ges tet sein, jedoch ohne die silbernen Arbeitsflächen usw. mitzuzählen.

429 An all-stainless kitchen will be very impersonal. A touch of white c give it a more welcoming feel, without it loosing its brightness.
Une cuisine entièrement revêtue d'acier inoxydable résulte très imp sonnelle. Une touche de blanc lui donnera un aspect accueillant sa perdre sa luminosité.
Eine vollkommen mit Edelstahl verkleidete Küche wirkt sehr unpersö lich. Etwas Weiß lässt sie freundlicher wirken, ohne dass dabei Licht v loren geht.

430 Plastic paint can substitute for tile in some locations, providing moist resistance while also offering more color possibilities.

Les carreaux de faïence peuvent être remplacés par une peinture plasti-que, qui isole de l'humidité et offre une plus grande variété de couleur.

Die Kacheln können durch normale Plastikfarbe ersetzt werden, die die Feuchtigkeit fern hält und mehr Möglichkeiten für die farbliche Gestal-tung bietet.

1 In small kitchens the color of under-counter cabinets should be bright.

Dans les petites cuisines, il faut que les armoires soient d'une couleur intense dans la zone située sous le plan de travail.

In kleinen Küchen sollten die Schränke, die sich unter der Arbeitsfläche befinden, eine intensive Farbe haben.

2 The overhead cupboards may also be painted a neutral color or lighter than the walls.

Une autre option est de peindre les armoires situées sur le plan d'une couleur neutre ou d'un ton plus clair que celui du mur.

Eine andere Möglichkeit ist, die Schränke über der Arbeitsfläche in einer neutralen oder in einer etwas helleren Farbe als die Wand zu streichen.

3 Warm colored sheer organza curtains give a romantic look to white-dom-inated kitchens.

Les rideaux d'organdi de couleurs chaudes donnent un air romantique aux cuisines dominées par le blanc.

Kleine Organzagardinen in warmen Farben sorgen für Romantik in einer weißen Küche.

434 In an L-shaped kitchen, a different color can be applied to the walls of the smallest space in order to create an office zone.

Dans une cuisine en forme de « L », on peut appliquer une couleur diffé-rente sur les murs de l'espace plus petit pour créer une zone de *office*.

In einer L-förmigen Küche kann man für die Wand des kleineren Bereichs eine andere Farbe verwenden, um so eine offene Sitzecke zu schaffen.

435 Plain white marble provides brightness and a sense of spaciousness.

Les sols de marbre blanc sans veines illuminent et agrandissent l'espace.

Weiße Marmorböden ohne Marmorierung machen den Raum hell und vergrößern ihn optisch.

436 A black-and-white check combination gives a traditionally detailed kitch-en a classic, elegant look.

L'association blanc et noir, à l'instar d'un damier, confère aux cuisines d'architecture ancienne, un air classique et élégant.

Die Kombination von Schwarz und Weiß im Schachbrettmuster macht alte Küchen klassisch und elegant.

431

Bathrooms
Salle de bains
Badezimmer

439

445

450

Waterproof paints are slowly replacing tiles in recent decorating trends as they offer a greater variety of colors.
Les dernières tendances remplacent les carrelages de faïence par des peintures imperméables, qui se déclinent dans une vaste gamme de couleurs.
Der neuste Trend besteht darin, Kacheln durch wasserfeste Anstrichfarbe zu ersetzen, die es in einer großen Auswahl von Farben gibt.

Stuccos are perfect for an elegant style when using intense colors.
Les stucs sont idéals pour utiliser des couleurs intenses dans un style élégant.
Stuck eignet sich ideal, wenn man starke Farben in einem eleganten Stil verwenden will.

The orange to white color range creates a spacious feeling and goes well with any type of furniture, regardless or its material.
Les gammes d'orange et blanc suscitent une plus grande impression d'espace et se marient à tous les meubles, quelque soit leur matière.
Gelb- und Weißtöne lassen den Eindruck von mehr Raum entstehen und passen zu allen Möbeln, egal aus welchem Material sie sind.

Mixing square tiles of different colors is a great idea for very small bathrooms.
Le mélange de carrelages carrés de toutes les couleurs est idéal pour les très petites salles de bains.
Die Kombination quadratischer Kacheln in verschiedenen Farben eignet sich gut für kleine Badezimmer.

441 Friezes make walls look smaller unless they are placed between two space-enlarging color zones.
Les plinthes réduisent visuellement les murs, à moins de les placer entre deux zones de couleur : dans ce cas elles agrandissent l'espace.
Zierstreifen machen die Wand optisch kleiner, es sei denn, man bringt sie zwischen zwei verschiedenfarbigen Flächen an, dann vergrößern sie den Raum.

442 To make a bathroom appear more spacious the walls should be the same color, but a shade paler, than the fittings and the furniture.
Pour que la salle de bains paraisse plus grande, il faut que les murs soient d'une même couleur, toutefois dans un ton plus clair que le mobilier et les sanitaires.
Damit das Bad größer wirkt, sollten die Wände alle die gleiche Farbe wie die Möbel und Waschbecken, Toilette und Dusche usw. haben, allerdings einen Ton heller.

443 If the dominant colors are cold ones, like blue, they should be balanced out by touches of warm colors such as orange or yellow. These can be provided by objects like towels, soaps, etc.
Si les couleurs froides, comme le bleu dominent, il est nécessaire d'avoir un contrepoids chaud : l'orange ou le jaune, pour serviettes, savons, etc.
Wenn kalte Farben wie Blau vorherrschen, muss ein Gegengewicht in Form einer warmen Farbe geschaffen werden, z. B. Orange oder Gelb für Handtücher, Seifen usw.

449

444 Shiny white tiles need contrasting colors.
Les carreaux de faïence blancs et brillants nécessitent des couleurs très contrastées.
Weiße, glänzende Kacheln müssen mit Kontrastfarben ergänzt werden.

445 If off-white is the dominant color, soft-colored furniture is necessary to achieve a warm, cozy atmosphere.
Mais si le blanc dominant est un blanc cassé ou ivoire, il faudra choisir un mobilier aux couleurs suaves pour créer une atmosphère accueillante.
Wenn das dominierende Weiß jedoch Eierschale oder ein gedämpftes Weiß ist, kann man Möbel in sanften Farben wählen, um eine gemütliche Atmosphäre zu schaffen.

446 The small surfaces of bathrooms are ideal for combining colors that lie opposite each other on the color wheel, e.g. yellow and blue.
Les petites surfaces de la salle de bains sont idéales pour marier les couleurs opposées dans le cercle chromatique, par ex : le jaune et le bleu.
Kleine Flächen im Bad eignen sich ausgezeichnet, um Farben, die sich im Farbkreis gegenüberliegen, zu kombinieren, z. B. Gelb und Blau.

447 Glass partitions visually enlarge the spaces they are in.
Les paravents en verre agrandissent visuellement ces espaces.
Trennwände aus Glas machen diese Räume optisch größer.

448 All that is required to separate the shower area from the other fixture areas in a medium-sized bathroom is to use colors that are next to each other on the color wheel.

Si la salle de bains est inintéressante, il est conseillé de séparer la che du reste des sanitaires en utilisant les couleurs voisines dans le cle chromatique.
Wenn das Bad mittelgroß ist, sollte man die Dusche durch den Gebra von Farben, die im Farbkreis nebeneinander liegen, abtrennen.

449 Graphite finished or very brightly colored fixtures increase the vi impact of the walls.
Les sanitaires décorés de graphisme ou de couleurs intenses ac tuent l'impact visuel des murs.
Wenn man Waschbecken, Toiletten usw. wählt, die mit intensiven Far oder Grafiken geschmückt sind, wirken die Wände stärker.

450 Black bathrooms are more elegant with a matt finish, such as graph
Les salles de bain noires sont plus élégantes avec des revêtem mats, comme le graphite.
Schwarze Bäder wirken eleganter, wenn man matte Verkleidungen zum Beispiel Graphit wählt.

437

Children's Rooms
Chambres d'enfants
Kinderzimmer

454

451

451 Colors in children's rooms must maintain a delicate balance betw
stimulation and tranquillity.
Les couleurs des chambres d'enfants doivent maintenir un délicat é
libre entre la stimulation et le calme.
Die Farben der Kinderzimmer sollten immer ein sanftes Gleichgew
zwischen einer anregenden und einer beruhigenden Wirkung wahre

452 In spaces that tend to be untidy the use of many different co
impedes harmony.
Dans les espaces où le désordre règne, la coexistence de nombrer
couleurs différentes empêchera de créer un sentiment d'harmonie.
In diesen Räumen herrscht meist Unordnung und es treffen viele Far
aufeinander, so dass nie der Eindruck von Harmonie entsteht.

453 Combined with white, bright, full colors contrive to give a child's roc
modern look.
Associées au blanc, les couleurs vives et franches créent une chan
d'enfants moderne.
Kombinationen mit Weiß, kräftigen und vollen Farben lassen ein mo
nes Kinderzimmer entstehen.

454 To break the monotony created by pastel colors, it is necessary to re
to small, bright surfaces (curtains, cushions).
Pour rompre la monotonie engendrée par les tons pastel, on peut re
rir à des petites surfaces (rideaux, coussins) de couleur intense.
Um die Monotonie, die durch Pastelltöne entsteht, zu unterbrec
kann man kleine Flächen (Gardinen, Kissen) in einer starken Fa
gestalten.

It is better to avoid protective bars as they make the walls appear smaller.
Eviter de préférence les barrières car elles rapetissent les murs.
Man sollte Zierstreifen vermeiden, da sie die Wandfläche optisch verkleinern.

Combining all of the furniture into a single structure (painted the same color as the walls, to lighten the room) frees up space for playing.
Concentrer les meubles dans une seule structure (les couvercles peints dans la couleur du mur allègent l'espace), permet de gagner de la place pour jouer.
Wenn man Möbel wählt, die in eine einzige Struktur integriert sind (wobei die Abdeckungen die Farbe der Wand haben, um den Raum leichter wirken zu lassen), wird Platz gewonnen, damit die Kinder spielen können.

Small rugs in harmonious colors are a fun and cheap way of marking out different play areas.
Disposer divers petits tapis de couleurs harmonieuses est une manière amusante et économique de créer différentes zones de jeu.
Wenn man verschiedene kleine Teppiche in harmonischen Farben auf den Boden legt, kann man auf preisgünstige und fröhliche Art verschiedene Spielzonen schaffen.

Pale stripes make a very small wall look bigger.
Les rayures aux tons clairs permettent d'agrandir la surface d'un petit mur.
Horizontale Streifen in hellen Farben lassen kleine Wände größer wirken.

Vertical, multicolored stripes on the wall opposite the bed give a child's room just the right touch of color.

Sur le mur opposé au lit, les rayures verticales multicolores confèrent à la chambre d'enfant la bonne touche de couleur.
An der Wand, die dem Bett gegenüberliegt, geben vertikale bunte Streifen dem Jugendzimmer genau die richtige Menge an Farbe.

460   To add height to a room, one of the walls and the ceiling should be painted the same cool tint (green, blue or lilac).
Pour accentuer la hauteur des chambres, peindre un mur et le plafond du même ton froid (vert, bleu ou lilas).
Um die Höhe eines Raumes zu vergrößern, sollte man die Wand und die Decke in der gleichen kalten Farbe streichen (Grün, Blau oder Violett).

461   If part of a wall is painted with matt black chalckboard paint, it is important to use a cool color, such as acid green, for the rest of the walls.
Pour créer un tableau noir, on peut peindre une surface en noir mat, à condition que les murs soient d'une couleur froide, comme le vert acidulé.
Wenn man eine Fläche an der Wand mattschwarz streicht, um so eine Tafel zu schaffen, sollten die Wände eine kalte Farbe wie Gelbgrün haben.

462   Large toy boxes will look less imposing if painted in light tones.
Les grandes boites pour ranger les jouets semblent plus légères une fois peintes en tons clairs.
Wenn man die großen Kisten, in denen die Spielzeuge aufbewahrt werden, in kalten und hellen Farben streicht, wirken sie leichter.

453

Work Areas
Zones de travail
Arbeitsbereiche

466

463 Unified colors and light furniture that blends well with the background visually enlarge working zones.

Pour agrandir l'espace des zones de travail, il convient d'unifier les couleurs et de miser sur des meubles légers qui se fondent au décor.

Um die Arbeitsbereiche optisch zu vergrößern, sollte man die Farben vereinheitlichen und auf leichte Möbel setzen, die mit dem Hintergrund verschmelzen.

464 Stimulating colors may be used for a work area that is in its own separate room. However, they should not be too strident.

Si l'aire de travail se trouve dans une pièce indépendante, on peut recourir aux couleurs stimulantes, tout en évitant les teintes criardes.

Wenn sich der Arbeitsbereich in einem unabhängigen Raum befindet, kann man anregende, aber nicht zu grelle Farben wählen.

465 One way of delineating a work area that is part of another space in the house is to make its shelving, desk and chairs a matching color.

Intégrée à d'autres espaces de la maison, cette aire peut être délimitée en utilisant une même couleur pour les étagères, la table et les sièges.

Wenn er in andere Bereiche der Wohnung integriert ist, bietet sich an, den Arbeitsbereich abzugrenzen, indem man alle Regale, den Tisch und die Stühle in der gleichen Farbe gestaltet.

466 Providing a visually uncluttered work space helps the user concentrate and work well, so mixing unrelated colors is not recommended.

Garder l'espace ordonné visuellement facilite le travail et la concentration. Il est donc déconseillé de mélanger les couleurs sans aucune relation entre elles.

Wenn der Raum visuell geordnet wirkt, macht dies die Arbeit und Konzentration leichter. Deshalb ist es nicht ratsam, Farben miteina zu mischen, die keine Verbindung zueinander haben.

467 Colors such as orange or brilliant green create a dynamic environm which combines perfectly with the dull metallic finishes of comp equipment.

Les couleurs comme l'orange ou le vert brillant créent une ambia dynamique qui se marie parfaitement aux couleurs métallisées des é pements informatiques.

Farben wie Orange und Mittelgrün lassen eine dynamische Atmosp entstehen und passen ausgezeichnet zu den metallischen Farben Computer und anderer Geräte.

468 Although beige and white are perfect with any style, they should dominate in spaces that require intellectual stimulation.

Si le beige et le blanc sont parfaits pour tous les styles, il est décons d'en faire les couleurs prédominantes dans les zones qui doivent st ler l'intellect.

Auch wenn Beige und Weiß fast zu allen Stilrichtungen passen, is nicht ratsam, dass diese Farben in Zonen vorherrschen, in denen die intellektuelle Anregung sucht.

469 Colored office equipment such as storage boxes, filing cabinets desk covers can be attractive elements of the decor.

Le matériel de bureau de couleurs, à l'instar de boites, classeurs et tection du plan de travail, permet d'attirer le regard.

463

Buntes Büromaterial, wie Kästen, Aktenschränke und Schreibtischaufla-gen, zieht die Blicke auf sich.

Clear-plastic file holders maintain a chromatic unity and, at the same time, give touches of color by letting the contents show through.
Les boites en plastique translucide sauvegardent l'unité chromatique tout en apportant des touches de couleurs, puisqu'elles permettent d'entrevoir le contenu.
Transparente Kästen aus Kunststoff sorgen für eine farbliche Einheit, aber auch für mehr Farbe, da manchmal der Inhalt durchscheint.

Metallic shelf supports look discreet while providing great storage space.
Les colonnes de support métallique argent, visuellement légères, offrent aussi une grande capacité de rangement.
Stützen mit silbernen Metallstützen wirken visuell leicht und man kann mit ihnen viel verstauen.

A screen is useful for partitioning off a work space but, to avoid looking incongruous, it should be painted in the same chromatic range as the rest of the room.
Un paravent permettra de délimiter les aires de travail. Pour ne pas dénoter, il convient de le peindre dans la même gamme chromatique que le reste de la pièce.
Mit einem Wandschirm kann man Arbeitsbereiche abtrennen. Damit er nicht wie ein Fremdkörper wirkt, sollte er in den gleichen Farben wie der übrige Raum gestrichen sein.

473 Yellow is one of the best options for the home office as it encourages creativity and stimulates thought.
À l'heure de peindre le bureau de la maison, le jaune est une des meilleu-res options. C'est une couleur qui nourrit la créativité et stimule l'esprit.
Gelb ist eine der besten Farben für das Heimbüro. Diese Farbe regt die Kreativität und das Nachdenken an.

474 Drawer units on castors will blend better if they are painted the same color as the primary piece of office furniture.
Pour que les tiroirs sur roulettes semblent s'intégrer à la table ou au bureau, il suffit de les peindre de la même couleur que le meuble principal.
Schubladenschränke mit Rädern scheinen in den Tisch oder den Schreibtisch integriert zu sein, wenn man sie wie das Hauptmöbel streicht.

464

474

Patios and Terraces
Patios et terrasses
Höfe und Terrassen

478

480

475

75 Direct contact with natural light allows the use of bright and intense colors on terraces and patios.
Le contact direct avec la lumière naturelle permet d'utiliser des couleurs intenses et brillantes pour les terrasses et patios.
Der direkte Einfall des Sonnenlichts lässt die Verwendung intensiver und glänzender Farben auf Terrassen und in Höfen zu.

76 Wood or rattan furniture combined with white or a natural stone finishes makes for an elegant, contemporary environment.
Les meubles en bois ou en rotin associés à des couleurs neutres comme le blanc ou la couleur sable, créent des ambiances élégantes et modernes.
Holz- oder Rattanmobel in Komblnatlon mit neutralen Farben wie Weiß oder Sandfarbe schaffen elegante und moderne Umgebungen.

77 In areas with little or no greenery, wrought-iron chairs and tables with brightly colored lacquer finishes provide an unusual counterpoint.
Dans les univers avec peu ou complètement dépourvu d'espace vert, les sièges et tables en fer forgé, émaillés de tons vifs, peuvent offrir une touche d'originalité.
In Umgebungen mit sehr wenig oder überhaupt keinen Grünzonen bilden Tische aus Schmiedeeisen mit einer emaillierten Tischplatte in kräftigen Farben einen originellen Blickfänger.

78 The shiny surface of plastic furniture gives more brilliance to complementary colors — orange, green and violet.
Les couleurs complémentaires — orange, vert et violet — acquièrent plus d'éclat et luminosité avec les meubles en plastique.

Komplementärfarben, also Orange, Grün und Violett haben mehr Glanz und Leuchtkraft auf Kunststoffmöbeln.

479 Nesting table sets make cheerful color combinations possible and do not take up much space when nested.
Une fois emboîtées, les tables gigognes, composées de trois éléments de taille décroissante, ne prennent pas de place et permettent de joyeux mélanges de couleurs.
Drei stapelbare Tische, einer kleiner als der andere, nehmen nicht viel Platz weg, wenn sie gestapelt sind und ermöglichen farbenfrohe Kombinationen.

480 Pots and planters used to define open-air spaces should be of the same color.
Pour délimiter les espaces à l'air libre, il est recommandé d'utiliser des pots et jardinières d'une même couleur.
Um Zonen im Freien zu begrenzen, kann man Blumentöpfe in der gleichen Farbe benutzen.

481 Neutral-colored hammocks and canopied settees are suitable for small patios and terrraces.
Hamacs et fauteuils suspendus, de couleurs neutres, sont parfaits pour patios ou terrasses de petites tailles.
Hängematten und Hängesessel in neutralen Farben eignen sich ausgezeichnet für kleine Höfe und Terrassen.

482 A display of cushions in the same color range enhances stonework or brickwork benches.

483

Un jeu de coussins dans une même gamme de couleurs, rehaussera les bancs maçonnés dans le mur.

Mehrere Kissen in verschiedenen Tönen der gleichen Farbe unterstreichen die gemauerten Bänke.

483 White sunshades and canopies not only reflect the light but also create an illusion of spaciousness.

Parasols et dais blancs reflètent la lumière, tout en conférant à l'espace une sensation d'amplitude.

Weiße Sonnenschirme und Baldachine reflektieren nicht nur das Licht, sondern sie lassen den Raum auch weiter wirken.

484 Multicolored rugs go well with furniture made of natural fibers. But aluminum furnishings require rugs of a single intense color.

Les tapis multicolores se marient à des meubles en fibres naturelles. L'équipement en aluminium requiert, par contre, des tapis d'une seule couleur intense.

Bunte Teppiche passen gut zu Möbeln aus Naturfaser. Wenn die Möbel jedoch aus Aluminium sind, sollte man einfarbige Teppiche in einer intensiven Farbe wählen.

485 Paper lampshades or warm glass lamps create an intimate ambience for those special summer evenings.

Les lampes en papier ou dotées de verres aux couleurs chaudes, forgent des univers intimistes, lors des nuits d'été.

Papierlampen oder Glaslampen in warmen Farben schaffen eine intime Atmosphäre in warmen Sommernächten.

486 Rooms that look out onto yellow-painted interior patios appear light and spacious.

Les patios intérieurs peints en jaune apportent de la lumière aux pièces voisines et semblent ainsi plus spacieux.

Gelbe Innenhöfe bringen Licht in die anliegenden Räume und wirken größer.

485

Decorative Elements
Éléments décoratifs
Dekorationselemente

491

487 Simple accessories can provide a splash of color and give personality to a monotonous, characterless environment created by a single, dominant tint.

Une seule couleur dominante engendre des pièces monotones et dépourvues de caractère. La note d'originalité peut venir de simples accessoires aux teintes contrastées dont la présence influe sur la nature des différents espaces de vie.

Die Vorherrschaft einer einzigen Farbe lässt den Raum monoton und unpersönlich wirken. Um dieser Monotonie entgegenzuwirken, kann man einfache Dekorationselemente in Kontrastfarben verwenden, die den Charakter des Raumes verändern.

488 Their light-reflecting ability makes colored glass vases perfect for dark corners.

Réfléchissant la lumière, les vases en verre coloré sont parfaits dans les coins plus sombres.

Bunte Glaskrüge reflektieren das Licht und eignen sich deshalb gut für dunkle Winkel.

489 Assorted cushions and plaids are ideal complements for a touch of brightness. Different textures can also enhance existing colors.

Le jeu issu des coussins et des *plaids*, en font des accessoires parfaits pour apporter une touche de couleur ou renforcer celles qui existent grâce au jeu des matières.

Die Kissen und Plaids sind ein ideales Element, um einen Farbtupfer zu schaffen oder die vorhandenen Farben durch das Spiel mit den Texturen zu verstärken.

490 Mirrors with large, white-painted wooden frames make small w appear larger.

Les miroirs aux larges cadres de bois peint en blanc sont parfaits p agrandir visuellement un mur très petit.

Spiegel mit breiten Rahmen aus weiß gestrichenem Holz eignen sich um eine sehr kleine Wand optisch zu vergrößern.

491 No longer considered luxury objets, chromed-metal accessories h become versatile elements that can combine with any style.

Accessoires chromés de couleur argent ne sont plus des objets de et se marient à n'importe quel style.

Kandelaber und verchromte Dekorationselemente bleiben nicht m einer luxuriösen Dekoration vorbehalten, sondern sie passen zu je Stilrichtung.

492 Red shaded lamps offer great contrast in pale, cool surroundings.

Les lampes à abat-jour rouge créent une bonne touche d'originalité d les ambiances aux tons clairs et froids.

Lampen mit roten Schirmen bilden einen schönen Gegensatz zu Um bungen, die in hellen und kalten Tönen gestaltet sind.

493 Halogen lights are best for illuminating pictures or paintings without torting their colors.

Pour préserver les couleurs des cadres qui s'illuminent *ex professo*, il préférable d'utiliser des lampes halogènes.

Um die Farben der Bilder, die beleuchtet werden, nicht zu veränd sollte man Halogenlampen verwenden.

489

4 The best place for plants with intense green leaves is opposite windows and other natural light entry points. It is a mistake to put them in dark corners.

Placer les plantes face à des fenêtres ou à des entrées lumineuses afin de mettre en valeur leur vert intense. C'est une erreur de les poser dans les coins sombres.

Pflanzen sollte man vor Fenstern oder dort aufstellen, wo Tageslicht einfällt, damit ihr Grün intensiviert wird. Sie gehören nicht in dunkle Ecken.

5 Rugs or floor mats with undulating stripe patterns tend to make floors look more spacious.

Les tapis aux rayures ondoyantes tendent à agrandir visuellement les surfaces qu'elles recouvrent.

Teppiche mit wellenförmigen Streifen vergrößern optisch die Fläche, auf der sie liegen.

6 One way of keeping dining room shelves tidy is by using storage boxes in a tone that matches the furniture.

Pour garder l'étagère de la salle à manger bien rangée, on peut utiliser des boites unicolores dont les tons s'accordent avec les meubles.

Um ein Esszimmerregal aufgeräumt zu halten, kann man bunte Kästen verwenden, deren Farben zu den Tönen der Möbel passen.

7 Stickers with designs that contrast with the color of the walls can be a helpful element in the decoration of monochromatic spaces.

Les stickers, aux motifs graphiques découpés dans une couleur qui contraste avec celle du mur, sont de bonnes solutions décoratives dans les espaces monochromatiques.

Aufkleber mit grafischen, einfarbigen Motiven, die zu denen der Wand einen Kontrast bilden, sind eine dekorative Lösung für einfarbige Räume.

498 Blinds and curtains that combine with any of the predominant colors of a room acquire character.

Stores et rideaux, en harmonie avec une des couleurs prédominantes des pièces, seront ainsi mis en valeur.

Markisen und Gardinen, die zur dominierenden Farbe passen, betonen die Wirkung dieser Umgebungen.

499 To help maintain the visual tidiness, and therefore the feel of spaciousness, in kitchens and bathrooms, it is important that the washcloths and towels be a matching color.

Pour contribuer à l'impression d'espace bien rangé, rendant cuisines et salles de bains plus spacieuses, il est essentiel que les serviettes et les torchons soient d'une même couleur unie.

Um den Eindruck von Ordnung zu schaffen und so Küchen und Bäder größer wirken zu lassen, sollten die Handtücher und Geschirrtücher die gleiche Farbe haben.

500 Neutral colored tablecloths make tables look smaller.

Les nappes de couleurs neutres réduisent visuellement la taille de la table.

Tischdecken machen einen Tisch kleiner, wenn sie in einer neutralen Farbe sind.

492

488

499

494

Design Credits • Crédits du dessin • Designverzeichnis

Alno AG
Alexia Sailer
88629 Pfullendorf
Germany
www.alno.de
15, 55, 125, 285, 428

B&B Italia
Strada provinciale 32
22060 Novedrate (CO)
Italy
www.bebitalia.it
135

Bisazza
36041 Alte, Vicenza
Italy
www.bisazza.it
203

Bonaldo
Via Straelle, 3
35010 Villanova PD
Italy
www.bonaldo.it
255, 247, 256, 393

Estudi Hac
Paseo Germanías, 12 bajo dcha.
46870 Ontinyent, Valencia
Spain
www.estudihac.com
36

IKEA
Plaza del Comercio s/n
28700 San Sebastián de los Reyes, Madrid
Spain
40, 47, 415, 453, 462, 485, 483, 480

Karim Rashid
357 West 17th St.
New York, NY 10011
USA
www.karimrashid.com
97

La Oca
Paseo Independencia, 19, 6.ª dcha.
50001 Zaragoza
Spain
www.laoca.com
72, 67, 65, 62, 113, 134, 204, 217, 232, 260, 261, 270, 279, 319, 337, 338, 386, 385, 402, 463, 474, 478, 489, 491

Rocher Bobois
18, rue de Lyon - 52 et 54
Avenue Ledru Rollin, 75012 Paris
France
www.rochebobois.com

Schiffini
Via Genova, 206
19020 Ceparana, La Spezia
Italy
www.schiffini.it

Tapeten der 70er
Rindsche Stiftstraße 38
61348 Bad Homburg
Germany
www.tapetender70er.de

Toscoquattro
Via Sila, 40
59100 Prato
Italy
www.toscoquattro.it

Zanotta Spa
Via Vittorio Veneto, 57
20054 Nova Milanese
Italy
www.zanotta.it

Photo Credits • Crédits photographiques • Fotonachweis

David Cardelús
229

José Luis Hausmann
297, 307, 322, 404, 423

Andrea Martiradona
390, 394, 409, 447

Luigi Filetici
369

Andy Birchall
39

Matteo Piazza
347, 368

Carlos Domínguez
83

Olivier Hallot
21, 372

Eugeni Pons
2, 181

Undine Pröhl
292

Giovanna Piemonti
433

Vercruysse & Owi / Dujardin
353, 363

Jordi Miralles
1, 453, 53, 123, 143, 162, 177, 178, 198,
205, 222, 242,301, 315, 312, 339, 450,
449, 456, 454, 451, 458, 464

Yael Pincus
260, 275, 423, 120, 229, 265, 308, 389,
424, 487

Jordi Sarrá
5, 7, 8, 12, 16, 17, 38, 48, 50, 51, 60, 75,
77, 94, 99, 100, 101, 111, 128, 132, 129,
140, 133, 146, 150, 154, 160, 165, 158,
159, 167, 179, 176, 182, 183, 193, 214,
211, 227, 226, 252, 266, 271, 281, 282,
283, 287, 295, 311, 306, 320, 328, 348,
356, 357, 379, 398, 395. 400, 414, 416,
417, 411, 413, 434, 445, 442, 439, 466,
475, 487, 488, 494, 499